Marketers Gone Wild

Networking and Schmoozing While Caribbean Cruising!

By
Some of the Worlds
Top Marketers

Dedication

This book is dedicated to all the Marketers
that have paved the way before us,
and the ones yet to come.

Table of Contents

Forward

Cruising and Marketers. Marketers and cruising. A match made in Heaven… or should I say the High Seas?

Cruising with 400 like-minded people that are in the same boat as you ☺, people that actually understand your business, people that you can actually talk to about your business, and having the opportunity to possibly Joint Venture with 20 or 30 or 100 other entrepreneurs, is something that doesn't happen every day.

The entrepreneurs that join this cruise every January are people that have been successful for many years, to those that have been in business a few short years, to those that are just venturing out. And it's an international cornucopia of the brightest minds in the Internet Marketing world.

Whether you're having a breakfast get- together, sitting at a table for 10 at dinner, or joining in on "Pizza and Profits" at midnight on the Lido Deck, you never know who you will meet and talk with. Secrets are let out of the bag, and some of the best relationships, business ventures, and friendships have been made.

We have been fortunate to have some of the best of the best share some of their greatest trade secrets for better business. Some of these authors charge thousands for this information through one-on-one coaching and consulting, but they have been kind enough to share their insights and expertise in this book.

This is a powerhouse of some of the best in the business, so kick back, read their "words of wisdom", and when you see them walking on the ship, having a drink at the bar, or lounging by the pool, tell them how much you enjoyed their story, and ask them what *you can do for them*.

See you on the Lido Deck for Pizza and Profits, or in the JV Jacuzzi!

Carolyn Lewis
"The Book Diva"

Chapter 1

The Importance of Mastermind Groups
By Mike Filsaime

Napoleon Hill, author of *Think and Grow Rich*, first defined the mastermind as a "coordination of knowledge and effort, in a spirit of harmony, between two or more people, for the attainment of a definite purpose."

For the last few years year I've been a member of 2 Internet Mastermind groups, one being the "Syndicate", with guys like Frank Kern, Yanik Silver, Brendon Burchard, and Jeff Walker, and one with Russell Brunson.

Since the publication of Think and Grow Rich in 1937, the idea of mastermind groups has grown and evolved into a staple tool for successful individuals. Napoleon Hill even went so far as to say there was a "mystical quality" created when a mastermind group was formed. He said: "No two minds ever come together without, thereby, creating a third, invisible, intangible force which may be likened to a third mind."

In other words, your ability to create things in the world is increased by having that invisible "third mind" of the mastermind group.

There are two basic types of mastermind groups: One which is focused on the success and vision of one individual, and one that is focused on helping everyone in the group.

Let's look at the first group. Andrew Carnegie's mastermind group was solely directed at his own personal vision.

Although he had over 50 men in his group, they were not there to discuss their own projects. They were there to focus on one, and only one main goal: the building of a steel empire. This was the vision *alone* for Carnegie.

The second type of mastermind group is one where all of the members of the group meet up to support one another in achieving a goal. These types of groups are everywhere, but aren't always named 'mastermind groups.' For example, a Weight Watchers meeting is a form of a mastermind group. This is where the members get together to *support each other* in their quest for getting healthier.

With 100% certainty I can tell you that being in mastermind groups has made a much larger impact on my business compared to anything else I've done. Why? Let's take a look at some of the reasons:

1. **Analysis** - You get the chance to surround yourself with a team of expert consultants that analyze your business, take it apart, and then re-build it to make it much stronger. They tend to see things that you are blinded to, and when put into action will help you take it to another level. That kind of independent analysis is extremely important because we all get too close to our businesses; we all assume we know the best way of doing something, when often there's a much better way that was staring us in the face all along – we just didn't see it.
2. **Accountability** - At each meeting you are expected to share your progress with the group. Without that accountability, you tend to roam free, and unfortunately things get done when they get done.

Knowing that you are answerable to the group for what you've accomplished since the last meeting is a strong motivator, and it provides the deadlines that many of us need.

3. **Joint Ventures** - As you get to know the other members, you'll start to see natural ways to work together and the partnerships that are created can be extremely useful. I've been able to team up with a number of members on projects where we've combined our strengths to produce and market all kinds of products and services.

4. **Positive Reinforcement** - When you surround yourself with successful people, you become more successful.

Recently I decided to start the Mike Filsaime VIP Mastermind Group. I have a lot of access to top marketers, and I wanted to be able to "spread the wealth and knowledge" that I have received from these amazing people.

This is an intimate group of serious marketers looking to not only get direct access to me, but to also help each other take their businesses to the next level.

As an exclusive member of the Mike Filsaime VIP Mastermind, you'll be privy to information that I very rarely share with others:

1. **VIP Email List** – You'll be able to communicate directly with me as well as the other mastermind members in open threaded discussions via a special private email list. This alone is easily worth the price to get in to this mastermind as this will keep you on

the cutting edge of what's going on in the industry and what's working right now.

There are already some super high earners (some doing 6 figures per month) part of the group all participating and sharing ideas, results, feedback...just about anything marketing related.

2. **Access To Mike's Personal Rolodex** – If there is someone in the industry you want to get linked up with to potentially do some business together (ie: get them to promote your product to their big list or interview them for your own product), I probably know them or know someone who knows them.

   And as long as you don't abuse this privilege, I will be more than happy to give you an introduction to whoever you want to get connected with – within reason, of course.

   I know all of the big players in the industry – guys like Frank Kern, Ryan Deiss, Russell Brunson, Yanik Silver, Brendon Burchard, Jeff Walker, Gary Ambrose and on and on – more than 250 easily – and will gladly help you get in touch with them one way or another.

   Obviously I will be screening these requests, but this alone could easily be worth the cost to get in the mastermind. Just think if you can get one of these guys to promote your product!

   The possibilities are endless.

3. **Access To All Of My Products** - By being a VIP Mastermind member, you will be getting access to all of my best products:

- **The Profit Platform** – partner up with me as an authorized reseller of this highly acclaimed print newsletter and grow yourself a steady stream of recurring income. Currently sells for anywhere between $497 and $1997 depending on how many site licenses.
- **Evergreen Business System** – by far the world's best automated evergreen webinar software. Now you can record a webinar presentation once, and run it on autopilot. All you need to do is send it the traffic and it does the rest. Builds landing pages, integrates with all major affiliate programs and autoresponder services, etc. It's a total beast, and the competition has been scrambling to pick up the pieces. Currently sells for $497
- **AffiliateDotCom** – Get access to the premier affiliate marketing coaching program I did with Chris Farrell. People paid as much as $1997 to get access to this training and many success stories have emerged as a result.
- **The MDC Monthly Newsletter** – Learn from some of the brightest marketers sharing their secrets month after month in my premier newsletter.
- Plus so many other products that are too numerous to add to this list!

The total value of the products listed above alone is well over $3,000 and they're all yours when you become a member of my Mastermind group.

4. **VIP Dinner with Me** - Whenever I travel, and I do a lot of traveling to various events all over the U.S. as well as around the world, both as a special guest and as a speaker, I will keep you informed of when and

where I will be, and you will be invited to a special VIP Dinner for mastermind members only. Feel free to ask me or anyone there anything you want to grow your business. Great networking and relationships will be formed at these VIP dinners.

5. **Open Office Mastermind** – 2 times per year, you and all the members of the mastermind group will be invited to my NY Office to spend 1 – 2 days to mastermind and brainstorm on each other's businesses to help them grow. There will also be time for fun stuff, too, like eating the world's best pizza, possibly going to Manhattan, etc.

   These types of get-togethers with like minded people all working towards similar goals and helping each other out is where MAJOR breakthroughs happen. Can't really put an exact value on this, but depending on how you harness this benefit could be worth several times the cost to be in the group.

6. **VIP Concierge** – 5 Days a week during business hours you will have direct phone access to a staff member on my team dedicated to making sure you are very well taken of regarding your exclusive membership to the Mastermind group. Whether you need help with anything listed above, from scheduling your consulting session with me, to getting in the mail queue to my affiliates for your offer, to when the next VIP Dinner is, my VIP Concierge will make sure you get what you need.

Plus you'll be connected not only with me, but also with all the other members who are serious about taking their business to the next level. Many of these members already earn anywhere from $5,000 per month to over $100,000 per month.

7. **Special Discounts On Products I Recommend To My List** – I promote a lot of great products to my list. From time to time, I'll be able to waive my commissions to work out a special deal for mastermind members only. Sometimes it will be a 50% discount (which is huge if the price is $997 or $1997). Other times it may be a $47 or $97 product that I can get the owner to let you get for free.

This one Bonus Perk will easily pay your mastermind access many times over.

Can you see the impact being tapped into a group like this can have on your business?

If you are truly ready to potentially add another zero to your bottom line, you need to be in a mastermind. Napoleon Hill said in Think and Grow Rich that every uber successful person he studied (these were tycoons of business) all were part of a mastermind and attributed much, if not most, of their success to being tapped into a group of people all with the same goals in mind and at the same level or on a higher level than themselves.

Being in a mastermind can help you achieve more than you ever will be able to on your own. Why not become a member of the most Elite Masterminds in Internet Marketing?

About Mike Filsaime

Mike Filsaime was born and raised on Long Island, New York, which he loves because of its four distinct seasons, as well as for its beaches, and the closeness to the Hamptons, Montauk Point and Manhattan.

Mike's early years were spent at Pathmark Supermarkets where he was in the frozen foods department. He also had a few other jobs while attending New York Institute of Technology.

His full-time profession was in the automotive field. For over 14 years Mike was in the retail end of the business, where he managed some of the largest auto dealers in the USA.

Mike actually started Internet marketing in October of 2002. His first purchase was a product called Instant Internet Empires, which taught him how to get started, and was really good for the newbie. But, he had to learn many of the other techniques on his own.

In 2004 Mike left his full-time job at the auto dealer. He started to pursue online marketing full-time, where he was able to achieve greater wealth online than he ever dreamed possible. Online marketing made Mike a millionaire in just 3 short years.

Over the years Mike learned a lot about marketing and sales experience in the automotive field. He handled much of the advertising for his dealership, and was also the head sales trainer for a 13 store auto group. At that time Mike took various courses on sales, negotiating, and phone selling skills. He has been able to apply many of the sales and marketing tactics he learned over the last 14 years and implement them into his Internet marketing.

Mike Filsaime's advanced strategies shook the Internet when he released the world renowned ButterflyMarketing.com. The Home Study Course made over $650,000 in less than 24 hours, and went on to produce 1 Million in sales in less than 5 days.

Mike is a student of How-To and Self- Improvement books, so he is always looking for that edge to take himself and his projects to the next level. He encourages people to be brave enough to purchase quality products that you come across that will enhance your life.

Mike is married and believes that the most important thing now is quality of life. A nice income makes it easier to have, but if you leave no time to enjoy it, you could be worse off than when you started.

You can contact Mike Filsaime at **mikefilsaime.com.**

Chapter 2

CRUISING FOR PROFITS?
Just Add Water!
By Capt Lou

Woody Allen said 80% of success is just showing up. It was way back in January of 2003 that I took his advice and attended my very first internet marketing conference called "The BIG Seminar" in Dallas, Texas.

I had hoped to learn how to put my local "Little Shop Of Cruises" travel agency online and reach out to a greater audience via the web.

Never did I imagine that the people I would meet there that weekend would profoundly change my business model, and the course of my LIFE!

It was another marketer in attendance that asked if I could arrange a similar event on a cruise ship, sort of a "seminar-at-sea" combined with a fun vacation vibe.

She asked if we could do mastermind meetings and JVs in a giant jacuzzi, sipping a pina colada, while sailing away from some sun-drenched island in the Bahamas or Caribbean?

Not even realizing that JV stood for "joint venture", I instantly said SURE, if you want to "cruise for profits"...JUST ADD WATER!

At that event, I bought all the info products and software packages and discovered how to automate the booking

19

process online, and how to finally stop selling one-on-one by phone, and start selling one-on-many through websites, webinars, live stage presentations, etc.

On Halloween weekend of 2003, my first "special-event-at-sea" debuted with about 50 students and speakers. We did just about everything wrong and yet it was a HUGE success.

It was that "Affiliate Marketers Cruise" that led to me transforming my business model away from one of a million travel agencies, to being a one IN a million producer / planner of specially themed niche group vacations.

Branding myself as "Captain Lou" the cruise-guru worked very well, and I quickly became THE go-to guy for niche marketers with audiences they wanted to WOW with an unforgettable, profitable and life-changing experience.

I started producing "Special-Events-At-Sea" for casino chip collectors, murder mystery writers, opera groups, multi-generational family reunions, real estate trainers, marketing coaches, consultants and gurus.

In January of 2007, I showed up again, at Mike Filsaime's $5,000 live event called the 7-figure Code. Mike has been a guest on some of our previous cruises and was starting to become more of a friend than a client.

His idea was to continue these cruises, but in a bigger way, with a much bigger vision.
The Marketers Cruise would be a no speakers, no selling, NOT a seminar-at-sea that is guru-student, but rather a true peer-to-peer networking and mastermind vacation that

would draw the world's TOP marketers for an adventure of a lifetime that happens every January.

Instead of adding a $1,000 to $5,000 event fee for attendees, which I do with many of my niche cruise events, our give back to the internet marketing community that has done so much for our businesses, would be to keep the Marketers Cruise at our costs!

Making it affordable, profitable and FUN for everyone to attend and bring their family and friends. The rest is history. Over the past several years, we've gone from 61 to 118 to 263 to over 400 attendees each January. Top VIP marketers who've put everything on hold to come join our cruise family include:

Mike Filsaime & Donna Fox (your hosts)
Robert Allen
Rich Schefren
Matt Bacak
James Malenchak
Russell Brunson
Ted Thomas
Joel Peterson
David Cavanagh
Jeff Mills
Daven Michaels
Joel Therien
Armando Montelongo

and many other top names including the publishers of this book, Mike & Carolyn Lewis, and the many entrepreneurial

CEO's who have contributed chapters about their personal marketing voyage.

The Marketers Cruise is my "flagship" product. It is what's turned "Captain WHO?" into "Captain Lou".

This event, where profitable deals are done while on vacation and having fun, has been the springboard for my Million-Dollar Groups System info-product, a $2,000 training course for cruise agents that has been flying off the shelves.

When I'm not speaking at travel industry events, I help develop groups for niche marketers who either want to bring their own audience on the Marketers Cruise or ANY cruise ship adventure to the Caribbean, Alaska, Hawaii, or Europe...instead of some stuffy hotel conference room.

Remember that to BE un-shoppable you need to be one in a million, not one *OF* a million. Carnival cruise lines have done a great job selling FUN. Make whatever you are selling an EXPERIENCE that's fun, and cool, with your own version of the "Champagne and Strawberries" at embarkation.

Your clients will never want to leave, and they'll keep coming back for more. Then one day, your industries' top leaders may tap YOU on the shoulders and ask if YOU would like to do a profitable joint venture with them, just like Mike Filsaime did with Donna Fox and Captain Lou.

Marketers Gone Wild

About Captain Lou

Captain Lou has 30+ years of sales and marketing experience, offline and online, b to c and b to b. He considers himself "psychologically unemployable". After getting fired 5 times in a row, Captain Lou built several 7-figure sales operations from scratch on little more than an 8th grade education and fire in the belly. His goals are to travel the world, not only fulfilling his own dreams and fantasies, but also those of his clients.

Captain Lou prides himself in showing niche group leaders how to cruise the world for free, with their own highly profitable "Special-Events-At-Sea".

He is the Creator of CruiseMarketingMagic.com and the Million-Dollar-Groups-System for travel sellers, as well as the Producer / Planner of the amazing annual internet marketer's mastermind and networking vacation known as: **http://MarketersCruise.com**

For more information, check out Captain Lou at: **http://CaptainLou.com** or

http://SpecialEventsAtSea.com

Chapter 3

Creating Your New Wealth & Freedom Lifestyle
By Daven Michaels

My entrepreneurial career started at the age of 15 with a dream to have a designer clothing retail store on Melrose Street in Los Angeles. Being so young I was turned down by everyone I knew for the start-up capital, so I turned to my supportive father for the money I needed.

My grand opening was a traditional Hollywood style fanfare, champagne flowing, cheers and slaps on the back. The days that followed were the most nervous days of my life! For the next few days I had no customers, not one! I recall feeling extremely anxious and worried; what if I had failed before I even started! I remember thinking about the money I had borrowed and how long it would take me to pay back my Dad. Even in those nervous anxious moments, in my heart I still knew I could make this work. I had to make this work. As fate would have it, by the end of first week Jack Nicholson bought out half my shop and I was in business! From that moment I knew I would always be an entrepreneur and I have never looked back.

I have truly lived the American Dream. I have turned multiple passions into prosperous businesses. I have been a bestselling music and television producer, author, speaker and successful entrepreneur. I have worked hard, played hard, travelled the world, and been involved with incredible people, amazing projects and exciting ventures. Some say I have been lucky, and maybe I have. However, very early on in my entrepreneurial career I became aware of a formula for success that I attribute my ability to turn multiple diverse businesses into financial success.

I first became aware of a success formula during my time as a record producer; I discovered that there is a formula for creating hit records. This made me think there must be a success formula for running a business. I actively sought out mentors who I knew were successful, and through their mentorship I developed a formula for success that I now teach to others!

In addition to running 123Employee, what I really enjoy doing is helping small business owners around the world create their new wealth and freedom lifestyle by showing them how to effectively leverage and delegate. Money alone does not translate into success. I know many rich people who are unhappy; they work long hours and are miserable. The definition of success, wealth and freedom are relative. My definition of success, wealth and freedom may be totally different from yours. My definition is simple; it's having the resources to live the lifestyle you desire, and being happy.

While I achieved financial success in my businesses early on, I did not achieve freedom and expansion until I fully understood and embraced how to effectively 'Delegate' and 'Leverage'. No successful person has been able to establish a business without mastering these two core concepts. Learning how to delegate is the bridge between self-employed and being a business owner, and yet, this is often easier said than done!

I think one of the reasons I am able to relate to "soletrepreneurs" and small business owners is that many of them tend to micro-manage, and I was one as well. Even today, my staff has to wrestle tasks off me, so I know how most people feel about hiring people to help them and then assigning tasks consistently to make an impact in the business.

Even though I manage a staff of 400 people, I still work from home. My management team and staff are all virtual, and I still consider myself a small-business owner, working with the same challenges as many entrepreneurs and small businesses who are my clients. Many key aspects of my business are delegated to employees all over the world, and this makes me uniquely positioned to share my experience with others.

Outsourcing is a form of delegation which is commonly understood as hiring people from countries like India, Philippines, and Eastern-Europe to do tasks for you. And while that is the common understanding, I believe we live in a global economy that is not limited by boundaries, nationalities, or cultures. When I use the word 'outsourcing' today, I think of assigning the task to anyone outside your company, regardless of geographical location.

Over time we have created a simple methodology for how to effectively create a delegation plan, which we call:

The 7 Steps to Successful Delegation

Step1: Deciding What To Delegate

The first step in creating a delegation plan is creating a delegation table for **EACH** project/income stream as follows:

1) Take a sheet of paper (landscape). Create 4 columns on a sheet of paper, and label as follows:
   - Column 1 : List the Tasks YOU HAVE TO DO
   - Column 2 : List the Tasks you HAVE TO outsource to others (you don't have the skill)
   - Column 3 : List the Tasks you are doing that could be done by others
   - Column 4 : List the Task you would be doing if you had more time or money
2) Divide the columns into 2 rows and label as 'Marketing Related Tasks' & 'All Other Tasks'
3) Enter all the tasks related to a project/income stream into the table.

Step2: Prioritizing What Tasks To Delegate First

In an ideal world it would be great to outsource EVERYTHING you don't have to do or want to do... the reality is that we are all limited by resources, and we have to prioritize what tasks to outsource first.

1) MUST OUTSOURCE NEXT

These are task or projects you MUST outsource next in order for your business to proceed. It could be the creation of a website, lead capture page, sales page, or copywriting. In most cases the MUST do list are things you are not able to do, or don't have time for and have to hire someone to do them for you. In many cases these tasks may be project based.

2) MARKETING TO INCREASE REVENUE

The next set of tasks I would outsource should lead to the generation of more sales. This would mean either:

- Hiring someone to generate more leads for you
- Delegating the bust task you are doing so that YOU can generate more sales.

We often advise our clients to implement an outsourcing strategy to hire someone to generate more leads via internet marketing, social media or telemarketing. While this might apply for many businesses, there are some instances where our client is a great sales person themselves and simply needs more time to make calls, attend networking events, talk at events, etc. In this scenario, we would look to identify tasks you are doing that can be outsourced so that you have more time to do what you are BEST at!

3) OUTSOURCE YOUR DISLIKE LIST, NOT GOOD AT & BORING TASK LIST

Once you have outsourced 'must do & marketing tasks', you can outsource your 'dislike', 'not good at', and 'boring and mundane' tasks you really do not want to do.

Step3: Selecting Who To Delegate To

Often new prospects will want to hire a $6 per hour VA, and what they are really looking for is a consultant, specialist or business/project manager. Knowing who to hire for the right job is crucial for your success. Once you have completed the table, assign the tasks to one of the following:

- **Consultant:** Someone who will advise you, create a strategy or plan of action. They typically do not do the work themselves.
- **Specialist:** Someone with specialized skills (graphics, web, technology, consultant, accountant, etc)
- **Business/Project Manager**: Manages key aspects of your business
- **In-house Employee:** Someone who comes into your place of business, full or part time
- **Remote Employee:** Someone who works remotely

Step4: Instructing How You Want The Task Done

Once you have identified the tasks to delegate, prioritized the tasks, and decided who to assign the tasks to, the next step is to create **B**asic **O**perational **S**equential **S**teps

The instructions should be simple, step-by-step, and easy to follow. If you do not know how to do certain tasks, ask your agent to research or review any applicable training material.

Instructions can be as simple as writing the steps in a word document, audio recording of phone calls, scripts trees, creating training videos and using screen capture software.

Step 5: Allocating When You Want The Task Done

In addition to providing instructions, we recommend you create a schedule and allocate time for different tasks throughout the week in Google Calendar or a similar program. This is often overlooked, often because you are too busy and don't have time to create the calendar for your employees. However, when the time is taken upfront, the results are improved.

Step 6: Understanding Why Outsourcing Might Now Work

Many people complain that outsourcing did not work for them, and they often blame their virtual employee or service provider. The reality is that there are six key aspects to outsourcing, which we refer to as the 6 pillars of successful outsourcing:

1) The business is not well defined or structured. The funnels, websites, copy, are not great...
2) The employers do not know how to communicate or manage, which overwhelms the VA...
3) The tasks are not appropriate for that level employee...
4) The instructions are not clear...
5) The employee/agent is not up to the task...
6) The employer has unrealistic expectations from their agent

When these reasons are adequately addressed, the better the outsourcing relationship will be.

Step 7: Know Your Role

Once you have made the decision to outsource and used the delegation process to decide what to outsource you will first need to get through the first 30-90 days. We do our best to assist our clients with this process. The reality is that they are YOUR employee working in our facility under our care and management. It is important you know your role in the process; they are your employee and will look to you for advice and guidance. Provide information and resources to allow their tasks to be done.

About Daven Michaels

Daven Michaels presents innovative marketing strategies to entrepreneurs and business leaders all over the globe year after year. Aside from being a dynamic business and personal development trainer, he is the founder and CEO of 123Employee, the premiere outsourcing center in the Philippines, with hundreds of employees working thousands of hours per day for freedom-starved entrepreneurs worldwide.

Daven is also the brains behind the 'New Wealth & Freedom' system, while also being an in-demand speaker. In addition, he travels the globe educating entrepreneurs about the benefits of outsourcing and the importance of delegation.

Many personal development trainers talk about making more money, working less, turning your passion into prosperity, having more time and freedom, and many sell great info products. Daven does more than talk about it, though: he has lived it, breathes it, teaches his success formula and strategies, and through 123Employee services helps entrepreneurs all over the world make more money, save valuable time and create the lifestyle they dream about.

Daven Michaels has been labeled a 'Super Entrepreneur' by

the media and his associates. Daven, who has been an entrepreneur since the age of 15, has enjoyed successful careers in the designer clothes retail industry, music promotion for crowds, and an award winning career as a music and TV producer.

Daven models the lifestyle he inspires, managing hundreds of employees with only a laptop and internet connection.

Now he devotes his energies to helping others discover the freedom of outsourcing as the CEO of 123Employee.

"One of the keys to success is 'Market Like M.A.D.' (Multiple Methods, Automation, Delegation)."
-Daven Michaels

Check out Daven at www.123Employee.com

Chapter 4

Information Marketing Can Provide an Independently Wealthy Lifestyle™
By Jason Myers

In my book "Independent Wealth Formula: The Ultimate Lifestyle Design System for an Amazing Life" I spend a great deal of time covering concepts to help entrepreneurs learn and live a formula for creating their vision and then living that vision to its fullest. You could call this a secret to "Living the Dream". One of the secrets to manifesting this lifestyle is to participate in events and networking opportunities like the Marketer's Cruise. Here's why: in today's information marketing ecosystem, you simply must be visible to gain massive amounts of traction in the marketplace. The traction enables a velocity that powers the achievement of the lifestyle. The traction comes from contacts, networks, joint ventures, cross-promotion and friendships within the industry. You simply can grow your business faster with people that share a common motivation than if you fly solo.

On the cruise, as during other networking events, there is a collective focus on growing and hatching new ideas for revenue. The most valuable part of the cruise is the sheer magnitude of time together. Think about this: I had several conversations with icons in the industry; people like Mike Filsaime, Brad Fallon, Russell Brunson and others. That would be epic for many info-marketers – period. What was amazing though, was a recurring theme with these folks; "Catch me anytime, I'll be here all week." Think about that for a minute. You're on a ship in the middle of the ocean with a captive audience of bright minds, successful marketers, multi-millionaires and they are captive and relaxed – all week. This, for me, was the part of the cruise that nearly seems impossible to replicate in a seminar format.

I have been in the information marketing business since 1997. I'm no newbie. I created a membership site in 1997 that made money its first month and I never looked back. I have exploited most every niche to make profits – for myself. I eventually founded and grew an online retail business to 1.865 Million products and 272 on the Inc. 500 list of the fastest growing companies. Then I sold that company to a public company that manufactured products we sold. Now my passion is to help entrepreneurs, using the lessons I have learned. This means I am like most info-marketers working on a new launch or product. I need people in the industry to get velocity. I am now building a new brand of information products, services, coaching, mastermind groups and experiential trips. There's plenty to do and plenty of networking and joint ventures to orchestrate.

My story of 15 prolific years in the industry might motivate some about the possibilities, while making others think I know everything - far from it. I have failed more than I have succeeded. Some of my successes have been very cool. Some of my failures have been epic. The key is to always get up, get going and keep your eye on the prize. I guess you could say that similar to other successful people, I have learned to learn from my experiences, the people around me and mentors. I know how to do "it" (whatever "it" might be) better next time. I think this is true for most people on the cruise. The depth and breadth of knowledge and niches was mind melting, rejuvenating and energizing.

I think you'll agree that entrepreneurs are by nature

optimists. They are most often thought of as married to their ideas. They are certainly married to the journey. It's a life's calling and there are always more ideas than time. There are always more opportunities than resources. This opportunity to resource imbalance is amplified by the format of the cruise. That's not a bad thing. You just need to know and manage it for success. On the plus side, I found myself creating what are very likely to be life-long friendships and business ventures. I hammered out joint venture deals during late night "Pizza and Profits" that'll be worth perhaps seven figures (yes, millions). I also found myself needing to wade through more contacts and follow up requests than any other event I have been to. This requires some sifting, sorting and strategy. My advice is to take copious notes during the cruise and to spend some time each day journaling. During this process you can organize and add thoughts to contacts and ideas that emerged that day before they leave your short term memory. When you get back to the "real" world, you can take massive action, as Tony Robbins would expect from you.

My belief is that if you are reading this book you have some desire to live the lifestyle. The internet marketing lifestyle, as it is commonly called. It is really an entrepreneurial lifestyle. For the 2012 cruise the cruise T-Shirt we all wore was very indicative of this lifestyle. It has three images arranged as a formula. I am partial to formulas, as you might guess.

The formula is:
Laptop + Lightbulb = Palm Tree

The palm tree is obviously an image of freedom. Here's my challenge to you: If you desire this type of freedom and recurring passive income, you need to surround yourself with like-minded people who are doing and doing it well. You owe it to yourself to learn, network and yes, even contribute to the community. Your life will be enriched in ways you cannot even imagine.

For some inspirational examples of living the dream, I'll share with you two very inspiring people: Katie Joy and Brian Ridgway. Katie Joy, the Global Butterfly, left a career as a Paramedic to design her ideal lifestyle. Her foray into information marketing is fairly new. However, she has trotted the globe masterminding and growing with people from every corner of the globe. Her information marketing business brings in cash whether she is on Necker Island with Sir Richard Branson or climbing Mount Kilimanjaro or on a cruise ship for 8 days with limited internet access. Brian Ridgway was working for Brad Fallon during last year's cruise and this year he joined the cruise after creating his own new high-end mentoring program. Brian moved to Hawaii and has created a recurring revenue stream that comes in while he is swimming, surfing or cruising.

Perhaps, these examples are too free spirited for you. That's fine. You must decide what lifestyle you prefer and then design your income streams to enable the achievement of exactly that. Katie has done it. Brian has done it. Countless other cruisers have done it. I have done it. I hope you have too. If not, let's get you on the path. In the Independent Wealth Formula, I delve deeply into the process to help you move from where you are to where you want to be. There is a formula.

You can have the lifestyle that is harmonious with who you are and how you want to live your life. If you are in the cubicle, you can move towards an independently wealthy lifestyle. If you are a stay at home parent, you can move towards an independently wealthy lifestyle. If you are a high school dropout or a college student, you can move towards an independently wealthy lifestyle.

My definition of this is a lifestyle independent of one source of income and independent of time spent on the income. It is one where you have scale and leverage. This means that you make money without trading hours for dollars. It means making money for years on work you did once, long ago.

When you hear about someone who is independently wealthy, it conjures various images in people's minds. I'm sure you have an image. One that I often hear is the "old money" image. Like an heir to the Rockefeller fortune, the Kennedy's, the billionaire's Sam Walton, of Wal*Mart, created in his family. You get the idea.

However, there is a new money, new economy version. This new version is what most successful information marketers achieve. It is a lifestyle with many streams of passive and active income. This passive and active income is where the power comes from and where the similarities to the "old money" are the strongest. Old Money knows that their money needs to bring them more money, without effort. As a new money person, you must develop several income sources to be independent of any single one of them. This enables you to have security and independence. It enables you to bring in revenue if you are working or playing. It allows you to maintain your lifestyle if you are working or hospitalized. It assures your family certainty, even if you get laid off.

Brendon Burchard was in Mexico and he wrecked an ATV. He

found himself in a Mexican hospital in need of surgery. His money was the last concern he had. You know why? He has passive, recurring income rolling in. He was able to recover, recoup and regain his strength and did not spend a minute worrying about his income, his medical bills or any of the "normal" things people in this same situation would worry about. He has independent wealth. He does not have old money; he is part of the new economy.

Do you think Brendon was giving his business 110% during his recovery? Heck no. In fact, in my book I dispel this common fallacy about this 110% idea. Truth is no one gives 110% to anything. You only have 100%. 100% is your best. 100% is your entire week. Let's look at this:

One Week = 7 Days = 24 hours x 7 Days = 168 Hours per week TOTAL

Now, you have to sleep. I sleep 4-6 hours most days. But, let's use 8 hours because that is what we should all get. That removes 8 x 7 = 56 hours. 168 Hours minus 56 Hours = 112 hours awake. Out of the 112 Hours left awake, remove 2 Hours per day to eat and 1 Hour per day for hygiene. This leaves 112 minus 21 = 91 Hours available for work.

Few people work 91 hours per week for their boss or for their own business. I could easily subtract hours for family responsibilities and commuting to your business or job or recreation. At a typical 40 hour workweek, you are providing less than 50% (40 of 91 hours) to your business/jobs efforts. Even at 60 hours you are only providing about 66%.

This whole exercise is to illustrate that you should not try to achieve or attain 100 or 110%. This is setting you up to fall short. Instead, I propose the following perspective: Design your plan for effort from the 0 Hours or 0% up. I would imagine that Brendon was at 0% during his accident and for a little while at the hospital and then he gradually ramped up as he improved his health. His income flowed, regardless. Yours should too.

Think about the paradigm shift here. At no time should you "have" to run at anything near 100%. If your lifestyle is provided for during short or extended periods of no effort, then when you really apply effort, imagine what you could accomplish in terms of explosive increases in income. Quantum leaps, surges of cash. Think of your income engine as having a big flywheel, that with each burst of energy begins to spin faster and faster and can spin faster between pushes. This is exactly how to design your income. Cover your lifestyle while in periodic coasting and then provide infusions of cash each time you "burst" your effort.

I hope this has helped expand your paradigm. Your time is now. Your business can be bigger than you can even comprehend today. You just need a system, some resources and a robust support network.

I am available for coaching, consulting and masterminding as you progress along this journey towards an Independently Wealthy Lifestyle™. You can learn more at

www.IndependentWealthFormula.com

About Jason Myers

Jason is a pilot, inventor, serial entrepreneur, author, and perpetual sponge for knowledge. He has founded countless successful offline and online companies since 1991.

His internet commerce experience began in 1997 when he launched one of the first paid online directory sites focused on professional speakers, trainers and coaches. He has launched multiple web businesses marketing to both B2C and B2B markets, including: magazine subscriptions, consumer products, motor pool software, GPS vehicle tracking, digital e-books, affiliate sites, shopping comparison engines, digital software downloads, pay-for-performance lead generation marketing, database-driven custom web applications (software as a service) used by Fortune 50 companies, and several other internet marketing endeavors.

In addition to his vast entrepreneurial experience, Jason served 11 years as an executive with Cingular/AT&T in various regional and national roles as a Director. Some of his largest assignments were to develop the company's five-year national sales distribution strategy, oversee its national retail operations for over 1,100 locations and 8,000 retail employees. He ultimately served as Chief of

Staff/D.O.S.O./C.O.O. of the company's largest operating market with a budget of nearly $2 billion annually, before he retired from wireless at the age of 34.

A forever self-proclaimed start-up junkie, he went on to co-found an online e-tailer with a catalog of 1.865 million SKUs to market in a low-touch business model leveraging proven drop ship, just-in-time inventory methods employed by Amazon.com, Target.com, and Walmart.com. As CEO and chief software architect, he achieved a rank of 272 on the Inc. 500 list of the fastest growing privately held companies in the U.S. He has since sold that company to a publicly traded manufacturer of consumer goods. He is the author of Independent Wealth Formula and founder of Independent Wealth Institute – an organization dedicated to developing entrepreneurs.

Chapter 5

Setting Up a Social Presence with a Content Cycle Strategy

By Miel Van Opstal

A lot of interesting content has been published about social media already, and many small businesses, entrepreneurs and professionals already have created accounts on quite a few social networks. There are hundreds of tutorials about each and every social network, dozens of statistics a week to check. The novelty factor of 'being present' clearly is long gone. Now it's the relevance and the content that matter. It's about affinity between your audience and you and about the frequency of interaction moments you have. With a good content strategy, you can recycle content and save time whilst maximizing your engagement.

It's all about creating a sustainable relationship with your fans, your customers, your stakeholders... This audience expects interaction, challenges and entertainment. The idea that social media is free is true when it's about basic membership. But even then you pay in time and content. For a couple of services you'll have to pay a small monthly fee to access some of the vital tools or statistics or you need to make a small investment, but in the end you'll see that these small costs were worth it.

Take some time to sit aside and think about who you want to reach online, what they are interested in and what you can offer to make people come to you for answers. Write down what kind of things you can offer on your website, how it should be displayed. Keep it as simple as possible.

Now think about what you want to achieve by starting a social presence. Do you need sales leads? Do you want to collect email addresses and start a list? Are you looking for people to attend workshops or seminars? What do you want to get out of it?

With a clear audience defined and a goal to work towards, it's time to set up a social hub with a purpose. You create content and interact on social platforms to drive people to your site:

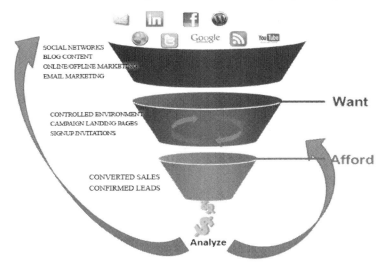

What you want to achieve is in fact that your Facebook fans, your Twitter followers or any member of social sites you're active on, all come to your website or one of its landing pages to follow instructions you provide to them. From 'Sign up here', 'Click here' and 'Register' to 'Read more' and 'Tell your friends'.

Let's imagine you're a small business owner and you need to start from scratch. The first thing you need is a domain name and some web hosting. If you want to have a lot of freedom, I suggest you get a WordPress install pack from the WordPress website. If not, look for a professional web designer.

Set up a website and create a blog. This will be the center of your content cycle. This is your engine. Create a nice page for your email subscriptions, or install some squeeze page to pull visitors into your conversion funnel. Gifts like whitepapers or research are often used in exchange for personal information. Think about what you would be happy with if you had to provide the information you're asking from your audience.

Now that you've created your own place on the internet, it's time to fill it up with content. We know more and more people are browsing the web with mobile devices like tables, slates or iPads. To make sure these visitors have a good experience on your website, download the free plugin OnSwipe and install it in your WordPress plugins folder. It will make the website a smooth, touch-friendly experience.

Next: make everything portable on your website. Everything relevant you post and share on your site should be made available for social sharing. Plugins like AddThis or SexyBookmarks will put Facebook Like, Tweet and Google+1 links and buttons around your content, making it easy for everyone to share what you have posted to their favorite social network.

Other free plugins you might want to take a look at: Yoast SEO, DisQus, Feedburner FeedSmith, Follow-Me. You need an Akismet anti-spam code too. You can get that by simply creating an account on https://en.wordpress.com/signup/. With all these plugins active and your design well in place, you can start to create content.

If you can't do some photo-shopping yourself, find someone who can help you to create nice profile images, a nice header for your website or logos and background images in the right sizes.

If you don't have a Facebook, Twitter, LinkedIn and YouTube account yet, now is the time to register and set it all up. Use the same style and images you're using on your website. Trust and recognition go hand in hand. There's a new social service that seems to be the big network of the year: Pinterest. You can create mood boards and pinboard walls with creative and inspiring content and share those.

With all your accounts set up and branded, it's time to create some synergy and make these things work together.

On your YouTube profile you upload all your videos and create playlists you fill with nice clips you come across. Make sure every minute you spend on YouTube is a 'signed-in' one. Send friend requests to people whose video you liked. Subscribe to their video channel and leave a comment. Bookmark everything remarkable you see in YouTube's playlist system. Each list can hold up to 200 movies. Create lists for 'inspiring videos', 'animation', 'cool commercials', 'funny', 'sports'... anything you're interested in. Then on your own pace, create a blog post for every video you like and write a small paragraph about what it is that makes the video interesting to you, and then connect it to something related to your business. Embed the YouTube videos and schedule these blog posts.

If you upload your own movies of customer testimonials, tips and tricks, interviews or reports, you can use the same strategy. Show the video in a context you control. Then add your banner to your product in the sidebar and below the comments, which fits in the conversion strategy.

Write some articles about what makes your service special, how your products can be used or why your insights matter. Every time you post an article, share the link to it on Twitter or Facebook. There are Facebook applications that automatically post to your page when you've updated your blog. If you use the NetworkedBlogs app, you can make it send updates to your profile or Page.

When you setup your Facebook Page, think about custom tabs and create a nice landing page. Look at what big brands are doing like Coca Cola or Mountain Dew, or the fashion industry. Make your page as attractive as possible and post polls, surveys or links to interesting content you've found elsewhere on the internet. Video & photography are great conversation initiators. If you want to, you can automatically send your tweets (or a selection of it) to a Facebook Page.

On your Twitter account, you have to become an expert in the things you represent. Find resources of your industry and curate evolutions, insights and reports. This is one part of your content. Find inspiring quotes from websites and take the time to select a couple of dozen. Schedule them in a Twitter client like HootSuite or Tweetdeck. Every couple of days add a quote. Between this, retweet interesting people you see around you on Twitter. Find people who 'like you' and see who follows them, then find the interesting people out of lists and summaries and follow at least 20 new people every day. Now every time you create content on your blog, tweet a link to that article.

Creative social networks like Pinterest or Instagram can help boost your traffic too. Be consistent when you register and make sure you brand your account as good as possible. Share content from these social networks on your blog (interesting collections you've created), then post links to the blog post on Facebook or Twitter.

You have to make sure that everything you do can be maximized. It's all part of a bigger project. What makes social media efficient is starting the adventure with a plan. Let's face it; we're all in this to make some money. It's ok to give and give, but there's no shame in admitting we're on the receiving end as well. That's why it's not enough to update profiles with a little blurb every once in a while. The updates need to be frequent and meaningful. That's the challenge, but it's the only way to succeed. If you have a plan to help you select the right content, it's much easier to maintain good social networks. Find me on a social network if you want to talk about this some more!

About Miel Van Opstal

Author and mobile & social marketing consultant Miel Van Opstal is an expert at helping small businesses gain a rock solid position in their local marketplace.

Miel Van Opstal specializes in helping entrepreneurs and small businesses gain a competitive advantage in their local market, both online and off.

Miel Van Opstal is a sub-famous social (mobile) marketing strategist and internet entrepreneur who helps brands, individuals and companies to connect with their target audiences.

Before his current job, he worked a few years for Microsoft as a Technology Evangelist where he traveled around the world speaking and presenting about Microsoft's newest online and mobile consumer products and services for technical and consumer audiences.

Currently, Miel works freelance for a couple of advertising agencies, a handful of small and midsized businesses, and for

Microsoft and some departments of the European Union. Apart from that, he sometimes gives guest lectures at colleges or universities.

If you are serious about improving your own business' bottom line, and would like to schedule a free consultation to see how Miel can set a comprehensive online marketing campaign for your company, you can contact him through **www.happymiel.be, or dial +32 472 675 692.**

Chapter 6

From Offline To Global Reach
A Non-Techie's Journey
By Andrea Woolf

What an amazing journey it has been navigating what for me were unchartered waters into this mysterious world of internet marketing. Until just over a year ago, having an internet presence seemed like a far-distant dream way beyond my reach. And I had no idea how to go about fulfilling that dream.

Before I get ahead of myself, let's go back in time to where it all started over fifteen years ago.

From the first moment that I discovered the field of coaching it was like finding the glove that fit me, uncovering my life purpose, what I'm truly here on the planet to do.

However, at the time I had a huge job in the worldwide corporate headquarters of Korn/Ferry International. So, being a smart woman, I hired my first amazing coach, Rick Tamlyn, to support, challenge, and keep me on track through the coaching training process and beyond.

Once I completed the training I was ready to launch myself on the world, but I heard myself asking, "Okay, great. You're a coach. So now what?"

How on earth was I going to find people to coach? Whilst the training from Coaches Training Institute was excellent, at the time there was very little about the business of coaching and how to actually grow your coaching practice.

Remember this was back in 1997. Whilst computers and technology were definitely blossoming, things were very different way back then. And since I'm so non-technical, it never even occurred to me to take the online approach! So my early efforts to find live human beings to work with were initially targeted locally.

Early in my coaching career I created the concept of 'Choosing Easy Over Hard.' In other words, if you had choice in the matter, would you choose easy or hard? I have posed this question to hundreds of audiences and clients, and only one solitary woman answered 'hard' – and it was because she misunderstood the question!

Of course I wanted to practice what I preached. In my quest to find people who would actually hire me to coach them, this begged the question: What would be the easiest ways to find those ideal clients?

The obvious first step was to share with people I knew what I was up to and ask them for their help. This actually took a lot of courage, since they would be entrusting me, this brand new coach, with their contacts. Magically, yet slowly, some started referring people to me, for which I was immensely grateful!

It didn't take long for me to want to spread my wings and meet more people. After all, I was the best kept secret in the Western hemisphere!

I learned that a very effective way to do this was to speak to groups. However, I had never done this before. Whilst I had a lot of experience on the stage, through acting, comedy improvisation, and even singing in various choirs, I had no clue where to start.

So I hired a second coach, specializing in "Public Speaking," to teach me how to do it. We had a lot of fun transforming me. As a full-blown perfectionist (I'm now a recovering one!), I started as a tense stick figure, clenched, nervous, and completely self-focused – worrying that I wasn't good enough, that I had nothing to say (of course not true), and no one would be the least bit interested.

With her help I learned how to focus entirely on the audience and engage them – and have fun doing so. I took to it like a duck to water because I love interacting with people. Very quickly this strategy proved to be successful, and I found new clients almost every time I spoke.

Next I was introduced to the world of networking, another business-building strategy that I hadn't experienced before. I focused in my local area, seeking out business groups. Again, since I love connecting with people, this was not only a successful approach, it was a fun and easy way to do it!

As all of my activity gathered momentum, I gradually established a local presence, as well as relationships all over the world. And as clients were delighted with the results they were getting in their business and personal life, they regularly referred people. This was truly a huge shift in my practice. It was a wonderful validation, and for me it represented that I had, to some degree, arrived as a coach. I'm happy and grateful to say that it continues to this day.

I feel truly blessed to have been doing the work that I love for over fifteen years. I work with amazing people to support them in growing not only their businesses, but also themselves, as they stretch and learn in their personal lives too, creating magical relationships, taking care of their health, powerfully contributing and making a difference, and remembering to celebrate and enjoy their life.

About three and a half years ago a gnawing feeling started to grow inside me to take what I was doing bigger. I knew that there had to be a different way to do what I was doing so that I could impact more lives and serve more people - and I realized that it would involve shifting my business model completely. But where to start?

I knew that I needed to learn new and different ways to design my business, as well as grow me to be ready to play much bigger. Out of the blue (although there are no accidents!) a great friend introduced me to Peak Potentials Training, led by the one and only T. Harv Eker.

From the very first program that I took, their Millionaire Mind Intensive, I knew for sure that I was in the right place. This was where I was going to uncover exactly how to do it. Over the next three years I took all of their programs and camps. I was challenged and stretched into not only acquiring new skills that I needed to take my business to the next level, but also expanding me and my internal conversation to prepare for that growth. I will be forever grateful for all of those amazing experiences.

It was during the same three years that I birthed and wrote my first book, *Ignite Your Life! How To Get From Where You Are To Where You Want To Be*. As I look back on it, it makes me both groan and giggle that it took me that length of time to go through the various incarnations that then became my book. It was my perfectionism that drove me to keep tweaking and editing, until I finally declared it complete.

As I look back on that time, it's miraculous that all of this was happening at the same time. I truly believe that it was no accident - that all of these elements needed to converge in order for me to get where I am now.

Now I found myself chomping at the bit to launch myself on the world. I had some ideas about how to do it, and a key element that was missing was to create an internet presence. Again, I came up against the wall of not having a clue how to do it.

Lo and behold, through one of my dearest and closest friends, Don Osborne, I had the great good fortune to meet Gina Gaudio-Graves, founder of www.DirectionsU.com, who invited me to join her Bachelors program.

It has truly been the most amazing, mind-shifting experience of my life learning all about and implementing her strategic approach to business and internet marketing, as well as mindset mastery.

I now have that internet presence that I dreamed of with my website, **www.IgniteYourLifeBOOK.com,** and am now reaching people all over the world every day. They are finding me, which I truly find miraculous! Through the system that I have learned and the power of keywords that they are looking for that I am using in my blog posts – and voila! our universes collide!

As I have been putting my website together over the last year and populating it with content, at the same time I have also been designing and launching my new business model, my group coaching program, so that I can serve many more people.

I'm also excited to share that the next launch will be my membership site, **Be The Ripple Now!** This will be all about helping people to reconnect with how much they do matter, then inspiring them to consciously take on creating ripples in the world, small or large. Coming very soon!!!

When I think about where I began and how different the possibilities are now through the global reach I now have at my fingertips, I am in awe of the limitless possibilities of it all. The future looks limitless and bright!

I am deeply grateful for all the guidance, training, love and support that I have received along the way from so many people. I surely could not have come this far without them.

And I am proud and excited to be a member of this wonderful internet marketing community. I look forward to continuing to stretch and grow and learn, and can't wait to share many exciting adventures together!

About Andrea Woolf

Andrea Woolf is an author, coach, seasoned trainer, and motivational speaker. Known as 'The Queen of Having It All', she loves to inspire people to do just that.

With her heartfelt style she has helped over 2500 organizations and individuals alike to clarify, simplify, and achieve extraordinary results, while bringing purpose and meaning to every aspect of their lives. Each day Andrea fulfills her dream of supporting amazing people in transforming their lives and truly connecting to the difference they make in the world.

Andrea has spent her whole life helping people identify what has been keeping them stuck and inspiring them toward living their most Ignited Life!

Growing up in London, England, while other kids could be found outside playing, Andrea preferred the company of adults. From a very young age, she would often be found at her mother's salon chatting with her clients as they were getting their hair done. Before they knew it, they would reveal their biggest challenges, and then commit to the action steps they would take the following week.

Communication has always been a passion and natural gift for Andrea, with an emphasis on what connects us rather than what divides us. She studied French and Spanish and achieved her combined honors Bachelor's degree from Queen Mary College, University of London. During this time, she had the good fortune to live in both countries. She then completed her post-graduate degree in Tri-Lingual Business Studies at the Polytechnic of the South Bank, in London, England.

Over the next 25 years, Andrea gained experience working in a diverse range of businesses at management level. She moved to the United States in 1979 and has called it home ever since.

Andrea brought her driven perfectionism to every role, and the expected standard she created for herself was to produce miracles every day. This would prove to be great training for Andrea in her role as a coach because what it took was absolute possibility thinking to pull it off.

From the moment Andrea discovered the field of coaching it was like finding the glove that fit her. She knew immediately that this was the contribution she was here to make. One of the first assignments Andrea completed with her coach was to design her transition out of the corporate world. Eighteen months later, almost to the date she had created in her vision, Andrea launched her coaching practice which has successfully flourished over the last 15 years.

In her first book entitled "*Ignite Your Life! How To Get From Where You Are to Where You Want To Be*" Andrea distills fifteen years of her experience as a coach. *Ignite Your Life!* was designed to help people go from settling to sizzling! It is a simple step-by-step system to clarify what is missing and to design and live the juicy life of your dreams.

To read more, visit her website at: **www.IgniteYourLifeBOOK.com**.

Chapter 7

Knowledge is Power

By Robert Puddy

How difficult is it to make money online? That depends on your perspective.

If you've been making money online for years, then you probably think it's pretty easy. But if you've never made a penny, then you may well think it's up there with rocket science and brain surgery.

The truth is that most things in life look complex... until you study them a little closer. Through study and practice, tasks that once seemed horrendously tricky, gradually become simpler, and simpler. Once you've been doing something for years, you tend to forget how puzzling it was to begin with, and you accomplish it without a second thought.

And yes, if you were to put this to a rocket scientist or a brain surgeon, they would most likely tell you exactly the same.

Think back to new skills and abilities that you've picked up over the years whether it's driving a car, learning to swim, or figuring out the remote control of your new TV. Remember how daunting they seemed at first, but how quickly they became second nature? The majority of the times, once you've learned "how", things are much, much easier than you think.

So when I tell you that making money online is simple, I don't say this because I've been blessed with some extraordinary

gift
or talent for manipulating the Internet to siphon money into my bank account. I learnt a way to make money online and I practiced, and I practiced, until it became easy.

Can it become easy for you as well? Absolutely! The only difference between you and me, at this point, is knowledge and experience. I can give you the knowledge and, if you practice what you learn, then you'll gain the experience as a matter of course.

If you're still doubtful, put me to the test.

One of the most common problems that budding online entrepreneurs run into is a lack of traffic. That's a pretty sizeable problem when you think about it. You could have the best product in the world and a sales page written by a copywriting genius, but unless you can direct a significant amount of traffic to your website, then your *PayPal* account will remain empty.

Your friends and family may be in awe of the website you've put together but then, so what. You're not trying to sell to your friends and family... unless you've become really desperate.

I think, at the very least, we can agree that traffic is a significant issue with which many people struggle.

Yet I'm willing to bet that, by the time you've finished reading JUST the next couple of pages, you'll have a totally new perception of web traffic, and you'll start to realize just how simple this really is.

Knowledge is power; read the next section and I can guarantee that making money online will feel a little easier than it did ten minutes ago.

Eureka Moment number one

Product + Traffic + Conversions = Money
They're not created equal

1. You can be really bad at creating products
2. You can be really bad at driving traffic
3. BUT if you're good at conversions you can still make shed loads of money

If you can't convince your audience to hand you money for what you are selling, No Matter how good the product...Or how many people you send to you're site

you will never make a dime.

~~Creating~~ Directing Traffic

If you're going to tackle the issue of traffic, the first thing you must do is understand the nature of the problem. This may sound like an obvious thing to say but I see many people struggling in this area because they haven't really thought about what it is they're trying to accomplish. Clear away any preconceptions you might have and just go with me for a few moments.

First, and most important, you must understand that the concept of creating traffic is a myth. Hence, the title of this section being called, not Creating Traffic, but rather, Directing Traffic. You may think this is merely a semantic distinction, but if you can truly grasp this concept it will open your eyes to the reality of Internet activity.

Web traffic isn't created; it's just a naturally occurring

phenomenon of the Internet-savvy 21st century. People all over the world are going online more frequently and for longer and longer periods of time. In fact, thanks to mobile Internet access, you could say that many people are online 24 hours a day.

The truth of the matter is that to truly CREATE traffic you would have to contact a person offline and then convince them to power up their PC, connect to the web, and then visit your website. Even direct marketing and telesales operations who aim to accomplish traffic creation in this way won't usually convince someone to drop everything and go online that instant. In practice, all they can hope to do is plant an idea in someone's mind so that, the next time they log in to check their email, they remember to visit the promoted website.

When marketers say they want to *create* traffic, what they really mean is that they want to re *direct* traffic to their website. At any given moment in time there exists Internet traffic made up of millions of people that are either surfing randomly or online for a specific purpose. Rather than trying to do the impossible and manifest visitors out of the ether, tap into these existing hordes of traffic and divert some of them your way.

Think like a hot dog vendor for a moment. Does a hot dog vendor set up his cart in the middle of nowhere and then send out leaflets hoping to attract visitors? Of course not! He goes where there is ALREADY an abundance of people, establishes a visible position, and starts pulling traffic his way. To begin with, most people will be on their way somewhere, and just stop to grab a hot dog before continuing on their journey. But eventually, some of the regular foot traffic in that area will start to go out of their way to buy a hot dog for their lunch.

There's a very good chance that you're not in business online to sell hot dogs, but the principle is the same. Find places that already enjoy a large volume of regular visitors and convince some of that traffic to make a stop-off at your website.

As a really quick exercise, grab a pen and paper and make a list of all the places you visit online more than once a month. Don't worry about making an exhaustive list, just scribble down as many as you can think of. Once you're done, read through your list and imagine yourself travelling through the Internet to each place on your list.

What you've created is an overview of the routes you regularly travel through on the Internet. Every person who goes online on a regular basis will be able to plot their own individual course. The purpose of this exercise is to try and visualize Internet traffic as a constantly moving stream of people, and start to think about how you can insert yourself into their field of vision.

The idea of trying to create as little as 100 visitors from scratch is a daunting prospect. But going to where there are already TENS of THOUSANDS of people and directing less than 1% of them to go your way for a little while? That sounds... dare I say it... easy.

A Solid Foundation

I've created, tested and catalogued dozens of different ways to successfully direct traffic, and they all have one thing in common.

They're all based on a single foundation, on top of which I sell products, build my mailing lists, and organize profitable joint ventures. Virtually every aspect of my online empire is constructed upon this specific strategy.

Would you like to know what it is?

As much as I would like to just come out and say it, if I do, I know that a small, but significant, portion of my readers will hurl the book across the room and refuse to pick it up again. Not because what I'm about to reveal is controversial, but because there are many assumptions and prejudices about this online platform that will lead some to assume either that this is going to be too difficult, or that they've already heard this one before.

So allow me to cut off these objections before they arise.

It's NOT difficult, and much of what you may already have heard is misleading or incorrect.

Before reading the next paragraph, please resolve to suppress any prejudices and hear me out in full. Ready? Here it is:

Every brick of my growing, and extremely profitable, online business, is built upon straightforward, but carefully designed... membership sites.

Whether I'm selling a product or service, building a mailing list of customers, or establishing joint ventures, using a membership site as the basis allows me to direct more traffic; and makes me more money up front, more money on the back end, more money from repeat business and more money from affiliate sales. It even helps me to arrange joint ventures with other successful Internet Marketers, even if they happen to have a larger mailing list.

I'm fully aware that this may sound like exaggeration or hype, but I really can't overstate the significance of the membership website model. Selling a product or service via any other method is denying your business multiple streams of income and opportunities to expand your online empire.

About Robert Puddy

Robert Puddy entered the online market place in 1999, lured by the promise of quick hard cash. He quickly realized that the hype was "nonsense" and that the online marketplace was no different from real-world business in that the same rules apply. "Sales is about meeting people and building relationships," he says. And this doesn't mean only in cyberspace. To promote his network, Robert manages to attend and hold seminars for Internet marketer's offline, both in the UK and the US. Through this work, he has learned that his talent is not just for selling, but also for training people to sell.

His passion is creating and supporting online network and mastermind groups. The rest of Robert's time is spent managing his multiple online businesses:

- ✓ **Net Learning Academy**   A coaching and training program, intended to bring all internet marketers into the 6 figure and above bracket using his Log in Frequency marketing strategies
- ✓ **Login Frequency Marketing**   The software developed to run my entire online holdings...and endorsed by some of the biggest names in IM

Check out Robert at **http://robertpuddy.com**

Chapter 8

How To Integrate Offline and Online Marketing So That There Is Synergy

By Bob Debbas

When a company starts out, before anything else, it is crucial that it has a brand name. This name must be short, distinguishable, and meaningful. One has to pick a name that is not offensive to another culture and translates well. Remember the Chevy Nova? This name did not go well in Spain or Latin America. Nova means 'it does not go' and who wants to buy a car that has that kind of name. Also, one has to pick a name that is available with a domain company such as Go-Daddy, or any other domain company that you choose.

Once you have your name, check to see if it is available as a domain. You'll want a good URL, and hopefully one that has the name of the company in it.

Now that the company has its brand name, it's time for the logo. Keep your logo clean and simple, and limit your colors to no more than 3. Not only will your logo look totally professional with a limited number of colors, (think Pepsi or Nike), but it will also be more cost effective when printing. Crowd source the logo to dozens, if not hundreds of designers, and then choose the best designer. Just imagine how much the client has gained by getting more choices. Check out MyGraphicsStudio.com, and add it to your list.

One final note on logos, always - always use contrasting colors. For example, use blue and orange, or red and white. You never want to use pink letters on a red background!

Make your logo stand out, but in a good way.

Don Shultz, of the Merrill School at Northwestern University, states that 'the center of all marketing communications is the customer'. Your message has to reach customers in many ways, and it will come from different places. Let's start with offline:

You only have 3 seconds to make a good first impression. A strong business card is a must when you are meeting and dealing with others. Clients will keep your card on file, so make it a memorable one. Besides the standard information of your company name, your name and phone number, be sure to include your Facebook ID, Twitter ID, and your QR Code (you can get this free on Google). Be sure to leave the back of the card blank for notes and messages. Check out http://www.weareprinting.com.

The next thing that a company needs is postcards. This is a great way to reach your target audience and is fairly inexpensive. You can easily buy 5,000 customized postcards for $250.00. (Check out WeArePrinting.com).

The important thing to remember is to customize your postcards, and perform a split test mailing. In the header of the first set, put something like "Free" and "Contact Jim". On the second set, use "Guarantee" and "Contact Tim". In reality, there is no Jim or Tim, but you will see which card has a better return. This will be the card that you will use for your mailings. The way to know this will be by the number of people who have called your company and have asked for either Jim or Tim.

Another way to reach consumers is to use promotional items. Know who your target audience is. Is it a man or a woman, young or old, tech savvy or not. If your audience is mixed, you can have one generic gift to give them, or you can have two. But whatever you decide, make sure it is new, fun and useful. For help with promotional items, check out
http://www.wearelogos.com.

If you are exhibiting at a trade show, buy a trade booth and bring banners, as well as a chair if one is not supplied, as you will get tired. Check out
http://www.tradeboothdisplays.com.

When putting graphics on the trade booth and banners, put your URL and Twitter account on them, as most clients have less than five seconds to look at your booth. Moreover, on the booth itself, write in bullet points no more than four to six words per line, and no more than three bullet lines. The important thing to remember at a booth is to get a potential clients contact info. Hold a contest giving away many products rather than one iPad. The reason is that more people will win, and more people will participate. The most important thing is the CRM (Customer Relationship Management), or follow up. A company exhibiting will spend between $4,000 and $5000K, depending on the booth space and the number of people they are taking to the show, in addition to travel expenses. Yet, it still surprises me how many companies never initiate a contact after getting a card from a potential customer. Just imagine the money left on the table when you don't follow up! Input your potential clients using CardsScan, or any other software that will allow you to keep in touch. This will allow you to email them with software like Aweber or Icontact. If not, there's no worth in exhibiting or attending a trade show. I remembered meeting Mike Lewis years ago. I kept in touch with him for years not knowing how we will work together, and now here we are collaborating on a book. What is important these days is to keep the relationship going.

Let's move to online marketing. Of course, small businesses will not use TV or radio, but could possibly do classified ads, as they still need to get themselves out there. Here again, the small business needs to test, and insure that the headline is tested. Some headlines can bring 18 times more response rates than others.

Of course the small business needs to make a website. The website should be user friendly. It should be fast to download. Be sure to have a lead capture on the site, as 97 percent of your consumers will not buy. Try to give consumers who are coming onto your website an ethical bribe. The bribe could be a promotional item. If it is a promotional item, say "Surprise". People love surprises. The value of a surprise is more than the item itself. It can also be a free eBook or a report. On the website, get as many testimonials as possible, but *real* ones and not fake. Have the person's name, title and company. If you want, you can also put their picture in. Keep in mind that video testimonials are a great way to draw attention.

I'll not get into SEO, or Search Engine Optimization, but I will say that link building is very important, as well as the Meta Tags you use. This topic can be another whole book, and there are already tons of books out there about SEO.

I'd like to briefly discuss social media. When I tell my

students about social media, I always tell them to beware because social media is not a business. What I mean by that is that social media is part of your marketing strategy, but Facebook , Twitter , LinkedIn , Google + , Pinterest , Foursquare, Highlight, and many more are a means to an end, and not the end. What every business should do is get involved in social media, and take the customers to the company's blog, or get the customer's emails. Why? Well, the truth is that if you have 40,000 fans on Facebook and suddenly Facebook decides to close your Facebook page, then all your work is gone. Of course, you should back up your Twitter and Facebook accounts, but still you will no longer have access to a two way communication with your followers, fans or connections. Now that we have a new Facebook timeline for Facebook, companies will need to ensure that the Fan page is done properly. Get involved in groups and other fan pages that are related to your fan page and post important articles. Then contact the group director and see how you can JV (Joint Venture) with him or her.

If we move on to Twitter, have a Twitter account whereby 8 posts out of 10 are information related and 2 are "soft sell". Give coupons on Twitter, which is easily done using different Twitter softwares. You can also poll your customers with a free tool called http://www.twitpoll.com, which gives you instant results for free. Moreover, followers love contests, and there are many ways to have contests on Twitter. When you tweet, tweet 120 characters rather than 140 so that you leave space to be re-tweeted. Moreover, you can tweet the same tweet 3- 4 times a day, as long as it is at different times so that you reach different audiences who are in different time zones. Always be positive. Tweet quotes. People love quotes, and it is inspirational. It is good to tweet a quote a day in the morning. On Sundays, people don't care to talk business. Look at the trends on the left and see what is trending. It might be something related to your industry and you can join the discussion. Use an application to find followers called http://www.twellow. When using it, know who your target audience is.

If one looks at LinkedIn, it is clear that LinkedIn is for the business professional. It is a very powerful social network that can be used for your company or for yourself. In the groups section, search for "Open Networkers" and join those groups, as those people want to network. Have a great profile. Use several keywords separated by commas so that when a potential connector wants to connect with you, and searches for a keyword, you are shown.

Although most companies are not using mobile yet, it is the killer app. There are more mobiles in the world than toothbrushes. The market of smart phones is expected to double every year for the next few years. With Foursquare as a business, you reward your most valuable customers. This is directly tied to the "Pareto Principle" which states that 20 percent of your customers will bring 80 percent of your profits. Moreover, users become mayors when they accumulate enough points and check in a certain amount of times to your venue. This creates a competition between users, and for mayors to keep their mayor status in order to receive gifts and rewards that are reserved for their special status.

One thing to remember is what the ex-girlfriend of Mark Zuckerberg said in the movie Social Network "On the net you write in pen, and not in pencil".

About Bob Debbas

Bob Debbas has been a serial entrepreneur since 2000. He started several companies in the US, including:

- *We Are Logos* : Promotional Item company that sells 750,000 items http://www.wearelogos.com
- *We Are Printing* : Printing firm that sells catalogs, postcards, business cards http://www.weareprinting.com
- *T-shirt Special* : Company that sells custom logoed t-shirts http://www.tshirtspecials.com
- *Trade booth Displays* : Manufacturer of Trade booth Displays and Banners http://www.tradeboothdisplays.com
- *My Graphic Studio* : Crowd sourcing company for Graphic and Web Designers http://www.mygraphicstudio.com
- *Weekly Interview:* Blog Interviewing Leaders. Goes out to 100,000 CEO's http://www.weeklyinterview.com
- *I Defend Myself* : Safety Product site selling Pepper Spray , Mace and Surveillance Products http://www.idefendmyself.com

Debbas is also a Marketing and E-marketing instructor to over 2,400 students at AUST and he taught at Notre Dame University. In addition, he has taught over 15,000 children how to use the computer, and worked with over 2,000 adults teaching them Microsoft Office.

Debbas is a dual citizen of both the United States and Lebanon, and speaks Arabic, French, English and Spanish. He is a Senior Foreign Correspondent to Arab Ad. He is also a member of Direct Marketing Association (DMA), American Marketing Association (AMA), Phi Kappa Phi Honor Society and Mortar Board. Adding to the many accomplishments of **Mr. Debbas**, he also attended the Clinton Global Initiative Summit 2011 in NY, and won the Takreen Advancement of Peace 2011 in Doha Qatar on Behalf of the Arab Spring.

Chapter 9

Networking At The Marketers Cruise..
How I Did It
By Warren Whitlock

There is always plenty to learn from speakers, but the best reason to attend events is the long term relationships that develop from interacting with other attendees.

This is why I love going on the Marketers Cruise. As I went through my preparation to network, I thought it would be interesting to document some of the ways why networking with speakers and attendees works so well for me.

Know Who Will Be There

As soon as I book a trip, I look for social media connections.

Let's start with a list of attendees:
- Mike Filsaime
- Capt Lou
- Donna Fox
- Tom Beal
- Brian D. Ridgeway
- Lasse Rouhiainen
- Joel Therien
- Ted Thomas
- Sharon Worsley
- Laura Betterly
- Mike & Carolyn Lewis

- Warren Whitlock (I know you'll want to meet this guy) ☺

I have been doing this for a while, so most of the attendees are already friends on and off Twitter. For the few that I couldn't recall, I used a Google search. Here is the syntax I use to find a user on Twitter using Google.

twitter.com "warren whitlock'
This all goes in the search box.

Google searches for occurrences of the text between the quotes on Twitter. Usually, you'll get only the most active use with that name. Click on the link, see the profile and FOLLOW the person. While on Twitter, be sure to read their recent tweets and click through to their blog and bio links.

Making a List and Checking it Twice (a day)

I created a list of these user handles to follow. I use PeopleBrowser, where I'll stack (column) open between now and a specific date to see what others are tweeting about. I've found that PeopleBrowsr is the fastest way to add people to a group, and it allows me to keep it outside of Twitter, where the limit to lists is only 20.

You can use a Twitter list (if you do, let me know and I'll refer others to it) or a group in almost any Twitter client for this. The Twitter search tool has improved; you may be able to find, follow, and list people as fast as the method I described.

Or, just follow this list I created: Marketers Cruise Attendees

I'll add other attendees to my PeopleBrowsr list as I find and follow them. The attendees list previously mentioned will likely be left as is to help you get started.

I use this for people I want to know better. I do not wait for them to start talking about the event, and actually prefer to find out what they are talking about besides The Marketers Cruise, since I want to have a relationship before and after that event. I already know we have that in common, so I look for what else we can connect on.

Building Relationships Before the Event

Using the links I get from Twitter feeds, I'll find links to blog posts about whatever expertise the person has, along with other interests on Facebook, LinkedIn and anything else they talk about.

What I'm looking for is their passion. I've learned that it's best to put off my interests for as long as possible and focus on what the other person needs and wants. Many of the famous people I network with are more interested in a charity, cause or avocation than you might think. Some might spend all their time talking about their niche or making money.. that's okay, but what I' really want to know is what passion they would follow if they had all the money they ever need. That's where the real connections lie.

Attack With a Preemptive Love Strike

Here's where the real fun begins.

Once you have spent a few minutes getting to know a person and their passions, you'll find at least one thing to love about them.

Now we get to put my *listen and love* marketing strategy into play.

Look for a question asked, a poignant comment, a shared life story or desire from the person you want to know better. I rarely need more than a few minutes to find at least one question or something to provoke a positive comment.

Now, do something nice for them. Instead of reading and thinking "that's nice", **TELL THEM** in a comment, tweet, or message. Please don't settle for "nice post" or "I'm a fan" (I use that when I'm nervous.. it rarely gets a positive reaction). Take a couple of seconds more and think of something *specific* and *personal* that you can say. It doesn't need to be long, but it has to show you really mean it.

My friend Dr. Ben Mack is calling this a *preemptive love strike,* which means that you don't wait for others to reach out to you, you **look for ways to show love**.

Since I've used Twitter and social media to help me show love and appreciate to others, I've learned to do it much more often... and now find ways offline to do the same.. handwritten notes, a book from Amazon with a note enclosed, a phone call when it's not expected.. I can't imagine ever running out of opportunities.

This works. I just set up a joint venture from sending one post card, I have sold consulting to someone who watched how I tweet positive ideas, and made new friends while strengthening bonds with many others from using these love strikes.

Watch for the HashTags

Attendees to the Marketers Cruise were encouraged to tweet and talk about the event and add a hashtag to the end of each post. This triggered a link in their posts and allowed others to click and see a stream of every tweet with that tag. They were also able to view this on the web using cool tools like TwitterFall.

TwitterFall allows you to click on a photo to see the current stream, or use the site to set up your own instant updating stream with whatever search term, with a list of people you want to see. It's great for projectors or monitors at events.

Using the hashtag, you can also set up a stack or column in nearly every Twitter client. On the web you can follow us from any browser with Twitter Search.

Attend the Chat Rooms

Anyone can attend the chat rooms to spend time with the attendees before the event. Listen to what they say, but watch for ideas of where you might send a preemptive love strike.

The Marketers Cruise chat rooms are available free online. Most other events offer similar pre-event meet-ups. When we do this, it's a preemptive love strike on attendees and many others who won't be able to make it.

Event promoters tell me that this doesn't hurt attendance. In many cases, attendance at these events go up due to people hearing about the event and deciding they want to get in on the best part.. the live networking.

Come to the Tweet Up

Many events have pre-events the night before the official start time. This is often the best way to get a leveraged fast start on meeting speakers, promoters and experienced attendees for a head start.

Go to Twitter and watch for announcements. When you see the invite, you'll be able to access a list of attendees and follow them.

By the time you get to the Tweet up, you'll already be seeing friends you met online.

Help Promote the Event

When you tweet about the event, you'll be doing a preemptive love strike on the promoter, the speakers and other attendees who will benefit from meeting you at the network.

This can be done even if you can't make it to the live event.

When you tweet about an event, point your followers to the appropriate website, and let them know the handles of the cool people who are speaking or attending.

This preemptive love strike is about as direct as you can get.

Keep in Touch After the Event

As you begin to use these tips, you'll find that it takes a lot less time than you might have thought before you start. Pretty soon, you'll have new friends and connections, a network of people that will remember your preemptive love strikes, and be looking for ways to help you.

It's natural to think that you have to sell something to them or perhaps it might be a waste of time. Actually, the reverse is true. The more times you can reach out and help (love) your contacts, the more apt they will be to ask you how they can help you.

When they do, be ready to engage them and move into whatever you need.

Of course, you want to keep your goals and desires in mind. I know we can't do an individual love strike on every contact every day, but I have doubled, doubled again, and am still increasing my capacity to do this. So far, I can't see any time that I will want to love less.

These are just a few of the quick steps I take when attending the cruise, or event a live event, and every day. I know each of these work because I'm using them. Do you have other ideas? Please share them with me. Leave a comment, Tweet about the cruise, and let's discuss what works and what hurdles you see. When you do, I feel your love 😃

Imagine a time when you'll have so many asking to engage you, wanting to reciprocate for the love you've show and anxious to see you do well.

Listen and Love.. it's as simple as that.

About Warren Whitlock

Warren Whitlock's mission is to help authors and businesses improve the results of their offline and online marketing programs.

Warren is a #1 bestselling author, speaker publisher, blogger, and social media marketing strategist.

Warren has been an entrepreneur in the computer, publishing and media. He started his career in broadcast advertising, developing cross promotions between two or more businesses, and has used the same strategies in direct mail and other media.

Over the past decade, Warren has taught thousands of small businesses, authors and individuals how to use proven direct marketing principles to promote product or service, started a trade association for manufacturers in the imaging products industry and served on several executive boards.

Chapter 10

The Mastery Of A Joint Venture Broker
By Muhammad Siddique

The most important element of doing Joint Ventures, or JV's, is having the right JV Mindset. You'll find doing JV's without it tends to become quite frustrating. But with it, you'll enjoy the process and the fruits of your labor.

Mindset is very important in this business. If you don't have the mindset of success, then you're destined to fail. Therefore, you need to understand the Law of Attraction, and utilize it to enable your mind, body and spirit to work in harmony for attracting and manifesting your desires and goals.

Anyone is capable of success if they put their mind to it, believe in themselves and take action to make it happen – even YOU! The Law of Attraction, when properly utilized, helps enable you with the proper mindset and strategies you desire.

Visualization is probably the best means of manifesting something specific using the Law of Attraction. In general, however, you may wish to generate a type of energy around yourself to continually be attracting certain energies that will serve you. For example, using affirmations can be very effective.

If you want to attract the energy of opportunity, then you could use an affirmation such as "I am the right person, in the right place, at the right time, doing the right things, with the right people!" This is a great one for manifesting beneficial joint ventures and joint venture partners.

If you want to attract joint venture opportunities specifically, you could use an affirmation such as "I am aware of and open to unlimited joint venture opportunities; I am involved in the best 'high-level' joint venture opportunities".

When you start doing deals, it is vitally important you start seeing yourself as someone who is on a mission to add value. You want to help others. You know exactly what your partners need, you know full well what would be of benefit to their clients, and you make it happen.

If you want them to feel something, you must feel it on a very deep level first. If you want them to see you as an expert, you must first see yourself as an expert. If you live it, breathe it and project it, doors will open and you will start seeing impressive results!

The Role Of The JV Broker

The role of the JV broker is a person who finds JV partners, sets up the deal and takes a percentage of the profits. You can make a lot of money by simply being a middleman or JV broker.

JV brokering is not a very difficult concept to understand. Just imagine an orchestra. Surely, such an ensemble wouldn't be able to play marvelous music without the help of a conductor. The conductor simply brings all the band members together and commands them how to proceed with a masterpiece. The conductor doesn't have to play any musical instruments; he just needs a good working knowledge.

The appeal of JV brokering lies in the fact that you can actually earn really good money by being one without having to create your own product, without having to employ any marketing strategies, and more often than not, without having to invest anything financially.

The JV broker essentially determines the type of resources the client needs, and works with the client to determine what can be offered to joint venture partners.

The JV broker also works out how to present the offer to joint venture partners where the prospective partners see the win-win situation.

Approaching potential JV partners in just the right way is vital to the outcome of the joint venture. The JV broker's role will be to assist the client when trying to convince people who have never heard of the client to enter into a JV deal through a well crafted JV proposal.

The JV broker has already determined what a potential JV partner can gain for the deal. They've done their research, they know who needs what resources, and they know how to find others to provide those resources.

I always tell people who ask me about JV brokering that in order to be a successful JV broker, a person MUST possess the following:

- A creative mindset

- A comprehensive and diverse network of contacts
- A good knowledge of your industry
- Good communication and negotiating skills
- A will to succeed

I can teach you the above, except however, the will to succeed. This needs to come from within you. Anyone else can try their best to bring out the competitive fire within you, but you alone must be able to conjure that fire and use it to your advantage.

Other roles of a JV broker include:
- Planning the joint venture
- Managing the complete joint venture
- Day to day operation, support and advice on the joint venture
- Reviewing terms of service
- Consulting with clients on joint venture partners
- Locating, analyzing and recruiting top producing joint venture partners
- Screening, reviewing and approving potential joint venture partners
- Monitoring and motivating underperforming joint venture partners
- Working with joint venture partners on improving conversions
- Reporting Issues and resolving potential problems
- Reviewing and assessing products/services from a marketing perspective
- Maintaining contact with joint venture partners,

handling all emails/calls

The Benefits Of Being A JV Broker

JV Brokering is such a lucrative and exclusive field. Knowing all the advantages you can derive in a career as a JV broker will develop within you a love for this job like I have. Loving your work is essential to your success, of course.

JV brokering, you see, is a highly creative business. It may not seem apparent right now, but trust me, there is more creativity involved in JV brokering than in any other field of marketing.

Let's look at some of the benefits that can be brought about by being a JV broker:

- You don't need to spend years building your customer list and constantly trying to build a better relationship with your subscriber base.
- You don't need to keep track of the sales made, of how much money is owed to whom, of fulfilling the product and sending it out, etc.
- You just step in, leverage those resources, and make colossal profits by bringing people together and contributing to others.
- You will be known as an expert that makes things happen and more opportunities will fall in your lap.
- As a JV broker your market is not seasonal in nature. Demand for your services runs the whole duration of each and every passing year.

- There will always be a need for a JV broker. For as long as businesses seek out fresh ideas to expand their enterprises and increase their profits, and seek out other businesses that compliment theirs, a JV broker will always be in demand.

Not only is JV brokering a great way of earning a fantastic living, it is also a marvelous way of positioning yourself as an established personality in the marketing field.

As a JV broker I have been approached by some of the biggest business gurus in the world to help them find JV partners, and also work on some lucrative joint venture projects just because there are not many JV experts available!

Imagine... if like me you're able to broker a gigantic deal that revolutionizes the industry because of its sheer expanse and the imagination that inspired it, you will forever be known as the mind that authored the project that people talk about for many years – you may even be invited to speak at some very 'high-profile' events worldwide like I do!

Marketers Gone Wild

Muhammad Siddique

Muhammad Siddique a.k.a Siddique is a Joint Venture Broker, B2B Sales Lead Generation Expert and Linkedin Strategist who produces results for B2B clients on harnessing social media and the digital space to bring brand awareness directly to businesses.

His work includes being a joint venture broker, marketing on Linkedin, Twitter, Facebook, Youtube and hundreds of other social media sites.

His core expertise includes:

- Joint Venture Brokering

- B2B Sales Lead Generation

- B2B Linkedin Marketing

- Social Media Lead Generation

- Social Networks & Joint Ventures

- Social Media Strategies

- Video Marketing

- Online Reputation Management

- Brand Management on social Media

- Social Media Campaign Management

- Local Marketing

Siddique partners with companies and creates new ways to grow revenues by leveraging hidden assets you have and you do not even know about.

siddique@trcb.com

skype id: siddique30024

http://facebook.com/siddiquefans

Chapter 11

Driving Traffic To Your Website

By César Fernández Nájera

In today's day and age the internet makes it quite easy for people to find the solutions they're looking for, but you can't expect them to just come to you; you have to meet them wherever they are searching.

Unfortunately there is nothing more maddening than trying to decide which online marketing strategies to use when you don't even understand them.

Believe it or not, there are business owners who avoid Internet marketing merely because they either don't think it's effective, don't think it's worth the money, because they've been burned before or simply because they don't understand it. However, none of these reasons are good enough to miss out on the opportunities that online marketing can bring to your business.

There are various online marketing techniques you can use to generate a continuous stream of new business that will allow you to truly connect with your local customers and prospects.

As consumer spending has taken a major decline over the past few years, connecting with your local customer-base is critical today. Therefore, business owners are scrambling for all of the business they can get. What better way to get new customers than to go where they spend a majority of their time?

You may be thinking, "Well, I have a website, so I'm already

95

'online.'" But a website is just one small step in the world of online marketing.

I do agree that having a website is an important step every business should eventually take to get an online presence. But are you *driving traffic* to your website? If not, what good is a beautiful website if it's lost in the dessert where no one can   see   it?

So in order to really connect with local consumers, there are several things you should consider. Once you are armed with this information, you will be able to implement solutions that will produce a steady stream of NEW and REPEAT local business!

Search Engine Optimization (SEO)

SEO is one of the most important ways to improve your profits, while reducing your advertising costs. While you can try to do SEO yourself, most businesses opt to hire a professional SEO firm to help them achieve faster results.

However, many business owners shy away from SEO thinking it's some huge monster that's going to eat them alive. Nevertheless, SEO is something that can help them generate more leads, customers, and sales for a fraction of the cost of traditional advertising methods.

SEO is a process of optimizing a website to improve search engine rankings. In a nutshell, this is the process of getting traffic to your website, which is achieved through "on-site optimization" and "off-site optimization."

On-site optimization should include the keywords that your business would like to rank for, as well as a few other key components.

Keyword research is the most crucial part of the SEO process because the keywords you target mean everything.

Get it *right* and you will see major results!!

Get it *wrong* and it will be a waste of time, energy and money.

You can do keyword research in the Google Keyword Tool. Simply enter your main keywords into the tool and review the results.

The results will show what keywords people are searching for, and how many times each keyword is searched for each month.
This is powerful information for you because now you know what keywords to target in your SEO campaign.

Off-site optimization involves getting relevant backlinks to your website, as well as establishing a strong presence spread out all over the Internet. This includes articles, press releases, videos, social networking, and any site other than your own. The more you have out there, the better.

All of these sources will contain a link back to your website that will help your website rank higher in the search engines, as well as giving you stronger online visibility. You can even create a network of "mini-sites" for your business that targets different keywords and links back to your main website.

Google Places

Google Places is a local business directory that allows you to profile your business and share information such as videos, photos, and hours of operation. This is an exceptional way to get great search engine visibility by listing, claiming, and verifying your business.

Google automatically lists most businesses in Google Places with very generic information - some of which is inaccurate. Therefore, it is extremely important for you to claim and verify your listing. This process will allow you to correct any inaccurate information, as well as share additional information about your business.

In order to claim and verify your listing, you simply fill out your profile and then submit it to Google. They will contact you via phone or postcard with a verification PIN number to activate your listing. You will then enter this PIN into your Google Places account to complete the process.

This powerful platform gives your business "credibility" in the eyes of local consumers. Complete Google Places profiles simply receive more attention than those that are not.

Google Places works 24/7 for your business, and is extremely mobile friendly. Mobile users are constantly searching for products and services in their local area while on the go. Google Places allows your business to come up right on their mobile devices.

Your customers can even get reviews of your business on your Google Places page. Even better, you can actually respond to those reviews and build a strong relationship with your customers. This will look good to people who find your page before calling you to do business.

Google Places business listings come up in search engine results when someone searches for your type of product or service online. In fact, Google Places usually gets more attention than organic listings when it comes to local products and services.

Usually, the top 3 results get the most attention, so you should strive to rank your website as high as you can. Of course, the **number one** spot is the ultimate goal.

If you decide to setup your own Google Places account, here are a few tips, just to recap:

- Be sure to fill out the complete Google Places page including pictures, videos, coupons, and any other information you can.
- Include relevant and accurate information about your business on your listing.
- Select the right categories when completing your listing for maximum effectiveness.
- Try to get as many customer reviews as possible. Offer something to your customers in exchange for them posting a review on your Google Places page.

Adding Your Ads

As you know, the Internet is all about "exposure." Since there are so many different online avenues when it comes to marketing, the most successful campaigns are those that contain a variety of methods.

In other words, don't use just one online marketing method... use several in order to get the best results.

Classified ads are also extremely important when it comes to SEO, and can be a very powerful marketing tool if you understand how to use it properly. Just like your website can come up in the search engines when people search for your type of service, so can your classified ad.

Not only that, classified advertising is affordable, targeted, and usually generates an ample response from local consumers. In addition, putting your website link in your classified ad provides a very strong backlink to your website, which in turn helps it rank higher over time. The more backlinks you have to your website, the better!

Banner Advertising

If you've been online for any length of time yourself, you've more than likely seen banner advertising in action. These are the graphic ads that you see on many sites. There are a number of ways to buy this advertising space. You can work with an ad network that handles the placement of your ads for you - choosing relevant websites, controlling what cities they get displayed in, etc. - or you can work directly with other websites to buy ad space on their pages.

You can even team up with other businesses in your local market to "trade" ad space on each other's websites. There are lots of ways to work with people who don't compete with you directly but would still be getting visitors who would be interested in what you have to offer.

For example, let's say you own a plumbing business. You

could partner up with local electricians, realtors, contractors and various other businesses to share ad space on each other's website. Someone who is looking for an electrician will quite likely need a plumber at some point, and vice versa. Someone looking for a realtor may be looking for a whole bunch of other businesses because they're moving to the area and aren't familiar with it yet.

This can even be taken a step further by offering "finder's fees" for any referrals that you get as a result of another local business. You can set up a system that will track any new customers who click through from an ad on one of your partner businesses' website and wind up contacting you. You can then pay the person who referred them a "finder's fee". If you set up these types of partnerships with several other complementary businesses, it can work out well for everyone involved, without taking anything away from their own bottom line.

Banner advertising can be very effective, but for local business purposes you need to be sure that you are able to control where your ads get displayed. If you're an electrician in Ft. Lauderdale, Florida, there's really no point is having your ad shown to someone who is surfing the web in Biloxi, Mississippi.

The bottom line here is that the internet gives you far better results than most traditional advertising methods. And it's not going anywhere, it's just going to become more and more important to local businesses as time goes on. If you aren't taking advantage of all the opportunities it offers, you have two choices - start taking advantage of them, or fall behind when your competition does.

About César Fernández Nájera

César Fernández Nájera was born and raised in Mexico City, and holds an Associate of Applied Science degree in Electronic Technology (graduating in the top 5% of his class with a 3.6/4 GPA) from T.S.T.I. - Waco, Texas.

From 1976 to 1978 he worked in the Qualtiy Assurance department of Radio Cristales Aztlán (a quartz crystal manufacturer) in Mexico City.

In 1978 he came to Houston, TX as a tourist with $800 in his pocket, looking to accomplish his dreams of becoming a Commercial Pilot and an Entrepreneur.

César worked as an Electronic Technician at Reliability Inc. from 1978 through 1993. He ranked highest in a class of 12 on the company's "Advanced Technician Training" course.

In 1988 Cesar became a Commercial, Multi-engine and Instrument rated Pilot.

In 1999 César founded AAA CDL Service, a school that helps people get their Commercial Driver's License, or "CDL", so that they can be qualified to drive heavy trucks, including 18-

wheelers for a living.

César became a U.S. citizen in 2000.

As an entrepreneur he has been involved in several industries such as Real Estate Investing, Mutual Funds/Stock Investing, Network Marketing, Internet Marketing and Truck Driving Instruction.

He is currently focused on helping businesses get more business with the help of the internet.

César is married to wife Adela and currently lives in Houston, Texas with their 2 Maltese dogs; they have no children.

For more information, you can contact César at **CesarGoingGlobal@aol.com**

Cesar's philosophy is this:

"Most importantly, I run my businesses with honesty and integrity. I do things that I am proud to show my spouse, family, and friends."

Chapter 12

Becoming Savy With Savvi
By Linda Boyd and Becky Estenssoro

When we embarked on our first Marketer's Cruise we really were not sure what to expect. Yes, we were told there would be life changing business and friendship connections, and wonderful opportunities, but we had no idea how much of a life-changing, truly rewarding experience it would be. It was a fabulous opportunity to connect with so many other marketers, all willing to share tips, information and encouragement.

At the first Mastermind Session we were fortunate to sit with Dave McGirr, a Founding Affiliate for Savvi. Intrigued by his elevator speech on stage we approached him and asked if he could expand on what exactly Savvi does and how it could help others. Dave was more than happy to sit with us and explain in detail how powerful Savvi could be to businesses, consumers, communities and non-profit organizations. We quickly became friends, and months later Dave is still supporting us as we rolled out Savvi in our communities.

Being a member of Savvi gives you access to 1 million deals from local, national and online businesses and you save up to 50% on the things you buy everyday!

We all know how effective Social Media Marketing, Mobile Apps, etc., are for local Merchants - - restaurants, cafes, salons, B & B's and others. The benefits of branding, lead generation, and advertising through social media help the Merchants promote themselves and raise their bottom line.

As hotels put bodies in beds, restaurants fill their chairs and other Merchants sell their products & services, money is pumped into local economies.

If as a marketer your bottom line depends upon selling these types of services then you will want to join us and Dave at Savvi. This is an unbelievable tool you can offer your clients, at no cost, to promote themselves. Savvi can open the door for you when approaching new clients. It's like giving away Girl Scout cookies and every Merchant you approach will love you for introducing Savvi to their business. Savvi can become a word-of-mouth engine for you as your happy Merchants encourage other Merchants to contact you for the incredible package of social media tools you offer along with Savvi.

Unlike other daily deals, Savvi is offered to the Merchant at absolutely no cost. The Merchant's deal is visible every day, not just one day. They can change their deal at no charge, and are encouraged to do so. Your Merchants, even small mom and pop businesses, appear on the same Savvi website and mobile app right alongside big national chains. Their logo is displayed in their ad to help with branding.

Savvi consumers don't have to purchase each deal, like normal daily deals; they pay a one-time monthly charge of $9.95 to access over a million deals each and every day from local, national and online businesses. They receive Savvi dollars and many other benefits. There's no coupon clipping for those Savvi consumers who have a smart phone and use the mobile app. The Savvi mobile app provides them with offers as they travel from zip code to zip code.

If you are not marketing local social media tools, but are involved in some way with non-profit organizations such as churches, women's shelters, the YMCA, or are involved in other fund-raising events, then you will want to introduce your organization to Savvi as an incredible fund raiser. Members can offer the great Savvi consumer benefits, a real value, and forget about bake sales, car washes, selling magazine subscriptions...and the donor will love the great Savvi deals and savings month after month as they continue to support your organization.

So join us today at **www.boomers.doyousavvi.com** or contact us for more details.

Another thing on our plate is Becky's Amazon Training Course - "Fast Track to Easy Street". Becky has been a Gold Merchant at Amazon for over 5 years and selling $500,000 plus of product a year on Amazon. Her expertise with Amazon, new research and assistance from our coach Joey Smith has transformed this Amazon course into the hot new product for 2013.

Amazon is THE Easy Street – the fastest way to giant profits using the world's largest global mall where opportunity, supply and demand can turn your internet sales into gold. There is no other Amazon course like this teaching you step by step every single detail to make you a success from budgeting, buying trends on Amazon, and sourcing products. Amazon is the ebusiness opportunity of the future. You will want to be selling on Amazon, or become an affiliate for this hot new product. The Kindle fire will be in the hands of 258 million internet shoppers by 2015, and they will be shopping on Amazon.

Becky and Linda will start conducting workshops for this hot new product the first of the year, as well as recruiting affiliates. Please contact us for more details.

Another huge project we've embarked upon is our Baby Boomer Brain Health website. The name of the site is www.BoomerNoodle.com – Vital Nutrients for the Aging Brain. This website is an accumulation of data, research and curated articles, advice and tips on the latest brain research for reversing your brain age and the risk factors to poor brain health. We've put together an extensive brain health glossary and resource section that covers brain fitness - games & puzzles, super brain foods, muscle for memory, brain enhancing supplements, alternative medicine, Zen for your brain, healthy body healthy brain and a whole ton more!

We've created a community online where you get the latest brain news about Anti-Alzheimer's Diet, Signs of Dementia, Supplements, and Activities to combat loss of brain function. We've also put together recipes and games to help improve your memory, exclusive interviews with well known people in the field, lists of the early warning signs of dementia, contributing conditions to poor brain health and a list of the risk factors of things that you can and cannot change in your life. The realm of information on this site is amazing! Come check us out!

If you'd like to be a part of our community or have anything you'd like to contribute to the site, please contact us anytime.

We'd love to have everyone on board!!

"Life isn't about waiting for the storm to pass...It's about learning to dance in the rain."

Warmest Regards,
Linda Boyd
Becky Estenssoro

www.boomers.doyousavvi.com
www.boomernoodle.com
www.babyboomerweekly.com

About Linda Boyd

Linda has over 20 years of marketing and sales experience. She also has had experience as the Downtown Revitalization Coordinator for Cashmere, a small town in Eastern Washington.

Linda created and managed a small cottage industry, Springdale Spa, a private label bath and body manufacturing company for several years. She's now promoting similar products on Amamzon.

She's also the Co-Founder & Creative Editor of **BabyBoomerWeekly.com** and **BoomerNoodle.com** - Vital Nutrients for the Aging Brain & Reverse Your Brain Age.

She's a Certified Joint Venture Broker who has gone through extensive training with world-renowned JV Broker Expert Willie Crawford, and entered the marketplace to work with clients in various niches.

Another huge project she's embarked upon is working with the Savvi Corporation as an affiliate. Becoming a member of Savvi at **Boomers.DoYouSavvi.com** gives you access to over 1 million deals from local, national and online businesses, saving you up to 50% on the things you buy every day!

About Becky Estenssoro

Becky has established many successful businesses. Her vast experience includes authoring several collectible books, an authentication service, online sales with eBay and Amazon, where she's been a Gold Merchant for over 5 years.

She's the Co-Author of a hot new product for 2013 - a Fast Track to Amazon, Easy Street to Giant Profits. This hands on Amazon training course like no other because of her experience and research.

Currently she's the Co-Founder & Senior Editor of **BabyBoomerWeekly.com** and **BoomerNoodle.com** - Vital Nutrients for the Aging Brain & Reverse Your Brain Age.

Prior to founding the Boomer websites, she was the co-author/editor/publisher of the BEANIE MANIA series of books, magazines and semi-monthly newsletter. Becky has also been a guest speaker on many TV and radio talk shows including CNN/Fortune, CBS News, CBS This Morning, Fox News, WGN, and has been featured in numerous publications including The Wall Street Journal, Time Magazine, Kiplinger's Personal Finance, and the LA Times.

She's a Certified Joint Venture Broker who has gone through extensive training with world-renowned JV Broker Expert Willie Crawford, and entered the marketplace to work with clients in various niches.

Another huge project she's embarked upon is working with the Savvi Corporation as an affiliate. Becoming a member of Savvi at **Boomers.DoYouSavvi.com** gives you access to over 1 million deals from local, national and online businesses, saving you up to 50% on the things you buy every day!

Chapter 13

The Do's and Don'ts of LinkedIn
By Randy Schrum

Social networking is one of the best ways to grow ANY business, and marketing is no different. In fact, social networking is a perfect fit for marketing when you think about it. Marketing is about "networking" – making a connection with other people. Social networking is doing that through the various online platforms such as Facebook, Twitter, MySpace, FourSquare and literally dozens of others.

LinkedIn is one such form of social networking. It's known as the ***professional*** form of social networking. And it is a GREAT way to grow your business.

Considering that LinkedIn is the "Suit & Tie" kind of network, there are quite a few things that you have to understand BEFORE you lose your privileges for being connected to this site, or any other Social Media Site for that matter.

Why Business owners Fail To Generate Leads Using Social Media Sites:

1) **Lack of Professionalism** – One of the reasons why the industry has been so watered down and overlooked is due to the lack of professionalism that many people display within the industry. Instead of treating it like a Multi-Million dollar organization, they tend to treat it like a side-hustler on the streets of New York City who's trying to sell cheap fake jewelry.

   The best thing you can ever do for your business is to treat it like it is a Fortune 500 company and command respect from those that you encounter. Perception is truly reality, and if you can get people

113

to perceive the value in your business, then they will respect it as such!

2) **The Opportunist** – What about that person that finds every opportunity to comment on a message or post with their business opportunity?? Hmmm... can we say annoying!!

   This is a very clear revelation of a person's inexperience and it screams "I'm a desperate newbie, you don't want to listen to me". True professionals are cool, calm and collective. Amateurs are incessantly promoting their business and constantly begging for a lead.

   If you want to be viewed as a professional, please don't do this!

3) **Lead with their businesses** – How often have you come across someone on a site like Facebook or Twitter that you just added to your network, and the first message they send you was a "check out my company, here's my website, tell me what you think" kind of message??

   That is such a turn off and one of the easiest ways to lose any sense of credibility. You should NEVER EVER lead with your business. You must first make the connection, then spend time getting to know your network, and later on, after you've established some type of rapport, you can "publicly mention" your business, but that still doesn't mean you send them a personal message about your business.

4) **Failure to show credibility** – When trying to earn the trust of strangers, you MUST prove yourself credible. The way to do this is to show your "expertise" about something. Whether you're a

great blogger, a technical geek or a Facebook expert, share information on something else other than your company. That way, you'll begin to position yourself as an expert within a niche that will help build your credibility!

5) **Talk about nothing other than their company and products** – There's nothing more annoying than someone who harbors on their company, the product and the comp plan over and over again as if they have no life outside of their MLM.

If you've been doing this, please stop! The way to engage others in conversation is to talk about things that are relevant to them, and if people aren't already in your business, it definitely won't be relevant to them.

It's okay to throw in maybe 1 or 2 posts that mention the power or benefits of being associated with your company or using your products, but make that only 10% of what you discuss.

If you can't find anything else to talk about, add motivational quotes, share relevant industry news and give people information about ways that they can enhance their lives personally!

6) **Spamming** – The biggest turnoff is when a fellow Business owner sends out a Mass message about their company to a huge list of people, and suggests that they get back with them.

Social Networks are designed to do one thing - socialize. And although there are lead generation opportunities within the network, you have to learn how to let prospects invite you to expose them to your business. Not be a forceful pesty salesman... if you do this, then you're equating yourself to that of a telemarketer, and you'll find yourself without much of a network.

7) **Abusing their Networks** – Following these points, the Amateur Business owner chases their entire network away. You'll find that no one will respond to their posts, comment on their pictures or even pay attention to anything that they do because they have officially disqualified themselves from being respected from their network!

Properly Generating Leads To You:

1) **Give value** – the secret to attracting leads to you is by:
   a. knowing your target market
   b. knowing what they want
   c. giving it to them!

In our industry, the perfect market that you want to pursue is "Other Marketers". Why?? Because these people are already sold on the industry, but most people lack success and are desperately in need of strong leadership.

The reason why most Business owners end up on the Internet is due to frustration. They're frustrated with:

- looking for ways to use the internet to get leads to join their business…
- spending more money than they're making
- tired of chasing after family and friends
- the lack of leads

What better way to position yourself as an authority figure, than to help those who are following in your footsteps. You may think that you're not experienced enough to lead other business owners, but the very same thing that you're doing through Social Media Sites, is the very same thing that you'll guide them on duplicating!

2) **Get to know your network** – Take time out to get to know people by participating in their groups, responding and commenting on their tweets, blog posts and videos and participate in their group discussions. This is the quick and easy way to get people to reciprocate your efforts. Give first, and they'll be more than happy to give back to you!!

3) **Seek to serve others first!** – If you find content and share it through various groups, in videos and in your blog posts that provide solutions to their lack of lead generation problems, then you'll be boiling over with a massive following.

   Seek to determine what people within your network need and give it to them first. Remember, we're here to provide solutions to people's problems and in turn, we'll find solutions to our own!

4) **Never lead with your company or company plan!** – It's okay to add your business into your resume in your profile, but do not pursue connections with people, and then send them a long email message about your company.... that's a negative!

5) **Show your professionalism!** – Remember, this is a Fortune 500 company, not some underground swap meet. Dress the part & Act the part, then you'll be able to Live the part!

Why your business needs LinkedIn

1. **It's networking at its best**

   ➢ You are connecting with other professionals, as LinkedIn is known as the Social Media Site for business professionals.

   ➢ You are connecting with people that you already know through a professional/school/work environment.

   ➢ You are asking THOSE people to introduce you to their professional connections, which turn cold leads into your warm market.

   ➢ This is NOT the "look what I did on vacation/my kids are so cute/my dog just had puppies" kind on connections. There is a time and place for that...but for your BUSINESS...this is where your real connections are.

2. **Customers** - Over 100 million people use LinkedIn – that's a LOT of potential customers!

3. **Sales** – There are several opportunities to connect with potential customers using LinkedIn, and you can also utilize LinkedIn to get referrals from satisfied customers to recommend you to other potential leads.

4. **Social Media** – there are ways to link to other social media sites such as Twitter and Facebook to fully integrate your social networking experience

5. **Events** – You can find out about events to help grow your business... and let others know about events you are participating in

6. **Recruiting** – There's a great opportunity to connect with new leads that aren't being spammed on LinkedIn with business opportunities like they

may be on Facebook & Twitter. It also allows your "professional side" to show more, removing your personal life from the equation, and giving you a chance to create a professional image.

7. **Build Credibility** – you can become an "expert in your field" by joining groups and participating in quality discussions

8. **Updates** - new applications are constantly added to make LinkedIn even better for your business!

LinkedIn Statistics

What do LinkedIn Users have to offer?

- Average Age: 41
- LinkedIn Users: Approximately 90 Million Users as of January 2011 in which 14 Million are Small-Business Owners.
- Household Income: $109,703
- College Grad/Post Grad: 80.1%
- Female Users: 36%
- Senior Management 16%
- Middle Management 18%
- Own Smartphone/PDA: 34%
- Business Decision Maker: 49%
- EVP/SVP/VP: 6.5%
- 24% Have a Portfolio Value of $250k+
- C-Level Executives 7.8%

Based on these statistics, you can see that LinkedIn is the most professional social media site, as well as one of the most underutilized sites for Marketers.

Establishing a dominant presence on LinkedIn will help you to create a great deal of credibility, and a new market of prospects that you can build quality relationships with, and eventually expose to your business.

About Randy Schrum

Randy Schrum has been fortunate enough to grasp enough about marketing that it has afforded him the opportunity to start, acquire, and grow inspired businesses. If you have an idea, struggling business or just not sure how to grow it, Randy is always open to explore it together. You can contact Randy at **randy.schrum@randyschrum.com**

Chapter 14

Millionaire Reveals Secrets of How to Make $10,000 to $20,000 a Day Closing Sales

By Ted Thomas

Nothing happens in a business until the sale is closed. No matter how well you perform during your sales presentation, if you walk away without the order, you have failed to do your job.

As A Business Owner- CEO or Entrepreneur

Putting your job in perspective translates to your number one objective as a business owner, CEO, or entrepreneur, which is closing the sale. If you don't close the sale, neither you nor the prospect benefits from your problem solving product. Bottom line, being a good closer is critical to your career as a business owner, CEO, or entrepreneur. Although closing the sale is the most important part of the selling process, it is an area that most CEO's are least likely to excel. Understandably, business people are in searching and seeking techniques and tactics to make their presentation more promotional. Later on I'll tell you about Ted Thomas' Famous Little Workshop - - Trial Closes; Statements and Closing Word Patterns.

Leaving Trial Closes to chance is a big mistake you don't want to take. Incorporating Trial Closes, you'll learn in this chapter, and using Closing Word Patterns, will improve the audience's appreciation of your message, and that newly established rapport and agreement with your message will create big sales numbers at the closing table.

Before we start and I give you actual examples.. Let's ask ourselves "what about your product?"

Let's face it, if your product doesn't perform and the product doesn't produce results, you need a new product. Does that make sense?? The customer wants solutions, so you must deliver results. When it comes to success, you're selling results; demonstrate and guide -direct clients and you'll be able to close the sale. Whenever possible demonstrate your results with testimonials.

What people really want and how to give it to them

People want to be richer, healthier, thinner, and more attractive to the opposite sex. They want to be more impressive to their friends, more independent, have more time that is leisure time, do less work, feel better about themselves, have interesting experiences, and raise successful kids.

Business people, entrepreneurs and presenters want a competitive advantage

Let's face it, the money goes to the speakers-presenters who know how to breathe new life into these old firmly establish wants of their audience. Knowing how to do this is a skill that you can learn, and when you do it right, it will give you a tremendous amount of power, because you'll become a source of new ideas and perspectives. This will allow you to have a competitive advantage over other presenters. As you incorporate Trial Closes, Statements and Closing Word Patterns into your client centric presentations you'll gain agreements early into your presentations. The client prospects will eagerly anticipate your closing remarks because you have addressed their needs and wants during your presentation. You'll need to do so gently and continuously, securing their agreements using Trial Closes throughout the presentation.

Your presentation - It's a performance... For example

Convincing and persuading takes time and requires you, the salesperson, to break down the presentation into easy to understand words and verbiage the customer can understand. That means ask questions and test for comprehension with Trial Closes.

Let's learn how

After you've made an important point that's beneficial to the client use friendly phrases like, "Is this making sense to you?" "Can you see yourself doing this?" These will require a response. It's up to you to gauge: is the response enthusiastic or does it seem forced? Keeping in mind, timid prospects won't tell you they don't understand; they don't want to look ignorant or be made to feel stupid, and they won't buy until they are convinced and they trust you. Assume they don't understand and keep it simple. I'll show you how.

If possible, demonstrate more than once, and get the customers, and when necessary the customer's staff, to be interactive. Be friendly, don't intimidate. Be sure the client/audience sees the benefits. Always understand that the presentation is a performance; it's educational, persuasive, and entertaining. That's what keeps customers engaged and interested.

You must demonstrate in a way that's exciting and easy to understand or you'll scare the customer away. This is a skill that needs continuous practice to improve the demonstration to be effective- demonstrations and social proof.

I'll give you a blueprint to follow

The compensation for salespeople is directly tied to preparation and performance. The salesperson is responsible for their own success. It's up to you to prepare the presentation with persuasive content that provides compelling reasons, methods that solve the customer's problems. Before I give you a few Trial Close examples to use after you've given customers your problem solving content, I want to remind you that it's important that this becomes your strength.

Trial Closes

I'm about to give you a huge gift of 7 easy to use, can't fail Trial Closes---crutches that will cause your income to soar!! When you finish presenting an important point say or ask---

1. You've got to get in on this.
2. Is this making sense to you?
3. How does this sound to you so far?
4. Let me see the hands of people who think this would be profitable for you and your family.
5. Would a deal like that create more security in your life?
6. Would your family be impressed with those kinds of profits?
7. Does your income embarrass you?

Customers want results - What's your track record look like?

The customer wants to know what results you and others are getting. This is your opportunity to make use of testimonials to demonstrate. If possible, make them visual using video, pictures, and graphics. The customer is taking the time to listen to you for one reason, and that's because they have problems. They will stay interested and continue listening only as long as you provide solutions. Salesmanship is a problem solving process that narrows down the problems and reveals solutions. The idea is to demonstrate solutions and relieve the customer's pain and close the sale. The customer will take action (buy) because you can remove discomfort. Your problem solving product presented with excitement and enthusiasm is...persuasion.

You start with a friendly relationship; ask questions that reveal the customers' needs, and then transition to the presentation. Assuming you understand the customer's needs, you're basically trying to move them from doubter, skeptic, to a new customer. Salespeople are in the business of customer development. In your presentation it's important to include SELLING WORD PATTERNS. These are used intentionally and multiple times throughout your presentation to drive home important points. For example: say within your presentations—

1. There's so much more I'd like to tell you- my time is so short- register and I'll finish up and give you more on the other side.
2. This is supporting your dreams
3. After a successful story, these are people I've impacted
4. My job is taking people from frustration to freedom

Why other people fail and you won't!

The number one reason why salespeople fail to get wealthy is simple. They don't understand USP (unique selling proposition). The secret formula for sales success is "be unique". I'll show you how. Add to that, you must offer solutions with products or services that no one else is offering. You'll learn segmentation and positioning. Most people go into a marketplace and offer what everyone else offers. That's going to get what everyone else gets. Keep in mind that sometimes it necessary to reposition your product.

Improve your pay day

I know you want more money. Then you must do more, which means you must be offering and doing what others won't do. Only the professionals ever put in the extra time to figure out the extras to make the sales see-saw tilt in their direction. If you want premium pricing or market leadership you must strive to make yourself unique by revealing more benefits and solutions and asking for the sale multiple times if necessary. I'll show you the process. **I'll give you a handful to use in your presentation.**

Lazy-means NO MONEY

Successful people always practice

The sales presentation when used by professionals is scripted and timed. A presentation that works is improved and refined again and again to bring in higher and higher results. Salespeople who are serious will add and delete segments of the presentation, depending on the audience and the economic news. Selling is solving problems and building trust along with credibility. Try to incorporate selling word patterns throughout your presentations.

Word patterns to incorporate in your presentation

In the age of skepticism, here's how to be a first rate presenter-speaker and close 600% more

          1. I'm going to take you to a safe place

2. I'll support you and continue to train you for 180 days-that's 26 full weeks
3. I'll keep you up to date and current on the latest FTC regulations- I'm going to fill you in on the truth
4. Folks, this is measureable and accountable
5. I have only 1 hour and 30 minutes to make a difference in your life
6. I want you to have more

It's all about "how to" get sales **now**, not next week. There's no fluff, no formulas, no long list to memorize, just "Trial Closes, Statements, and Closing Word Patterns" that will get the heads in front of you nodding yes. I recommend you start with one or two "Trial Close, Statements, and Closing Word Patterns" and later develop the remaining. With practice, you'll make more money quickly and easily.

Timing matters a lot

In selling, it's wise to ask for small commitments before you ask for the big one. The trial close process applies whether you're making a big ticket sale on the platform or you are out on a date with a hope towards marriage. There's a big difference between asking someone out for coffee the first time you meet and proposing marriage. In sales, as in marketing, timing is critical. By utilizing trial closes and securing agreements on small issues, it's much like going for coffee on the first date and then proposing dinner after you create rapport. Trial closes lead to the big commitment down the road but only after many small commitments have been secured. In sales, you must demonstrate and communicate credibility and believability. Then you trial close to secure agreement by patiently explaining the affect (benefit) of your product and what problems it will solve or what profit it will generate. This will go a long way toward creating believability and credibility.

And there's more...

Don't miss out on your share of the huge profits made from platform speaking and marketing your talk and products. The concept is:

Do something once and sell it over and over.

This simple concept can make you rich! Of course, most of us never find out about this little secret because they don't tell it in school. Instead, they tell you to study hard, get a good job, work till you are 65 and retire on social security. But, it doesn't work that way. Good jobs are tough to find. The government is broke and no one wants to work for a company until they are 65.

The secret is- do something once, and sell it over and over and over. Look at the rich in our society. They use this same formula. *Do something once and sell it over and over* formula.

This is the road to wealth. Information marketing is the road to wealth for ordinary people. It's not unusual for newcomers to go from rags to riches using this method.

It could be a single CD or DVD, maybe a booklet or a complete course. The quickest way I know to make a million dollars is platform speaking. In demand speakers have CEO's, Presidents and Sponsors begging to schedule them. Speakers keep 10%-50% of product sales. A $100,000 2 hour talk can easily net a speaker $50,000, and a recorded version brings even more. A speaker who builds a $35.00 course and sells via mail, TV, or radio only needs to sell 30,000 courses to bring in an entire $1,000,000.

If you only produce one CD a month and sell 350 copies, your cash flow will be $160,000 next year.

Keep in mind the major studios cannot afford to produce and distribute less than 10,000 CD's- you can! Your video won't be evaluated on the Hollywood Studio production value. The viewer will be evaluating based on content you gave from the platform at a seminar.

Once you learn - - -

My system makes it easy to make big money immediately and do it again and again. It's like making soup in a microwave: no complicated formula or ratios, no computer glitches. All you need is an audience and a microphone.

The entire process will fit in a UPS cardboard envelope, yet it makes more money in a month for those who learn how than a brick and mortar business like sub sandwich shops, pizza joints, muffler shops, hair salons, pack and ship, or even dental offices do in six months.

The ability to sell and close opens new worlds of profit
It's time for you to cash in on the most profitable field in the electronic and international world, and that's speaking, which usually includes publishing. It doesn't matter if you are 16 or 66, rich or poor, black, white or brown. You can make more money in one day than most people make in a month. It's an international world and we live in an informational age where there's big opportunities to learn and succeed as a publisher of your own information products. This will allow you to control your future and create a lifestyle for yourself that others only dream of. It's fun and it's a prestigious field

of work.

It's simple to make a personal fortune. All you have to do is sell your presentations. It could be reports, booklets, books, software, newsletter, CD's and DVD's. The profits from these sales will free you from the 9 to 5 rat race, and you won't need an expensive office. You can live anywhere – small town in the countryside or a condo in a high rise. It's not difficult to make a million dollars when you create the product and sell it over and over.

America needs your help

Across the USA 50,000,000 small businesses need help - how to make money, how to be sexier, how to be thinner. If you sell 25 units a day at $35.00 using the internet or classified ads or even direct mail you'll earn $183,750, and if you have several products your income would be on the top of the charts.

After spending 20 years developing profitable products and writing two best-selling books and developing dozens of complete courses and selling them in print, on TV and from platforms at large events and seminars I can help you turn your speaking empire into a self-publishing empire and avoid the mistakes that are wasteful and costly. It only takes common sense and a willingness to take what you already created and follow a step-by-step plan. It's not complicated. There are 50,000,000 entrepreneurs and small businesses that are hungry for information. You can find all your experts by using outsourcing.

In closing, I'll tell making the decision to be a "Closer" is going to change your life in many ways. Not just the new income you'll enjoy, there's so much more. When you persuade from the platform your self- esteem and confidence will soar. People will want to be next to you. Businessmen will look to you for your opinions and advice. You'll command respect and admiration wherever you go. This is a prestigious, looked up to profession that you'll be proud to be part of. Expect envy from those who won't invest the time and necessary effort to grow to the top of their game. Yes, your ego will be pumped up. Don't worry, your wife and kids will still know you as just "Dad" and they'll expect new cars and a bigger house, private schools, and the waiter at the best restaurant in the city of Paris will still think of you as another American – You'll know better when you add his big tip.

It's time to make everyone proud of you.

If you want the immediate income and prestige acquired from being a sales closer, you're in the right place. Closing sales is the "secret" to the large nest egg you deserve for you and your family.

About Ted Thomas

Ted Thomas is a Florida based educator, publisher and author. Thomas is a publisher and author of more than 30 books. His guidebooks on Real Estate have sold in four counties of the world.

In the recent past, over 75,000 clients have carefully evaluated Ted Thomas' *QuickStart Introduction In Secured Tax Lien Certificates* and have chosen to become associated with the market leader. Thomas' Home Study Materials are international best sellers and draw clients from Europe and South America.

After watching his parents work hard their whole life and die almost broke, Thomas decided it was time to dedicate himself to finding an investment strategy that would help senior citizens, as well as young people, avoid humiliation of not having enough money.

In two years of researching and traveling, Ted has visited thirty states and hundreds of counties. He has interviewed dozens of government officers and venture capitalists.

From that effort has emerged the most comprehensive program for low risk and high yield returns available in the U.S.A. These discoveries are almost hidden government programs that yield up to 25% interest. Surprisingly, these government-sponsored programs have been almost secret for decades.

Ted has developed in-depth training programs that show you step-by-step how to profit from tax lien certificates and tax deeds. He is the pioneer in teaching this material, and has been doing it for over 20 years. Thanks to Ted's dedication to educating people about this low risk high yield investment strategy, the secret is getting out. In-fact, more and more people are popping up on the internet teaching this material.

Sign up for Ted Thomas' Free online training webinar and begin learning to invest in tax lien certificates from the one educator who has been teaching thousands of people for over 20 years.

www.tedthomas.com

Chapter 15

Building Wealth Through Real Estate

By Tim & Janelle Johnson

Real Estate investing is one of the best ways to build up wealth.

There will always be businesses that will thrive in their season, and there are others that will thrive for the moment. Like everything else, there is a rise and fall in the real estate market in general. Even with that, you can still benefit from real estate investing. In fact, when the economy is *not* at its greatest, this becomes some of the best times for potential real estate investors to get great deals for investment properties.

When the prices of properties are lower, banks want to sell quickly. Another possible aspect about a sluggish market is that you still have some stability, even with a downturn in the economy. Don't think that when there are economic downturns, that it is the end of the world. It isn't. People don't realize that it is one of the best times to purchase property at an affordable price.

For those who are interested in real estate investing, this can be a great deal for those who can get in the market quickly to snatch up those homes and use them as rental properties. You just have to make sure that you are in the right place at the right time.

Generating Positive Cash Flow

When looking at real estate properties as financial

investments, you will have to decide whether an appreciated value or positive cash flow is your main goal for buying properties. Before you can make that decision, there are a few things that you will need to consider.

Since you would probably be looking at both single family homes and multifamily homes, note that there is a difference between the two. With the former, the value of the property usually increases in value quicker. However, since more expenses are attached, you may not be looking at the kind of positive cash flow that you want.

On the other hand, multifamily units (i.e., duplexes), can generate more positive cash flow. But, they may not appreciate quickly like single-family homes do, and there may not be as many expenses attached to the latter. Since most real estate investors look to create wealth, they will most likely choose having a positive cash flow. In this case, you will need a reliable real estate agent that is willing to help you find real estate properties that will produce the positive cash flow that you want.

Real Estate Investing Tips

I can't stress enough the fact that when you're starting out, don't rush into getting the first piece of property that you see. It's important that you conduct your due diligence. Even though it is a lucrative and profitable business, you can lose money if you don't work it properly. Look at the balance sheets and see what you will look forward to as far as repairs, maintenance, fees and other miscellaneous expenses.

Don't listen to all of those stories that you hear about people making lots of money "overnight" with real estate investing.

It can take weeks or months to actually get the property that you want, and it takes more than a day to start seeing a profit.

If you take your time and look around, you may be surprised as to how much is available to you in terms of real estate properties. There seems to never be a shortage of places where you can find a place to use for a profitable investment. But find a good real estate agent that is willing to genuinely help you. You may even be fortunate enough to find one that is also an investor on the side.

Now once you get into real estate investing, it's very important to stay in it for the long haul. That's the way you will create wealth. There are those who like getting their feet wet when the iron is hot, but when it gets cold, they want to bail out. Regardless of whether the market is up or down, you must be willing to weather any storms that come about.

Gaining lucrative wealth from real estate investing comes with staying the course. Let's take a look at some of the ways that can help you make real estate investing worthwhile:

- ❖ When you do decide to purchase property for investing purposes, seek counsel from those who have come before you. It's important that you have adequate information before you jump into something like this. Real estate investing involves time and money. You need both in order to make this business work for you, and you not working for it.
- ❖ Find experienced investors that are willing to spend time showing you some of the ins and outs of real estate investing. They can share some of their experiences with you and advise you on what to look out for.

❖ Try not to hoard a bunch of properties all at once. Start out with one and then work your way up. Working at a slower pace will help you to properly maintain and manage what you have.

❖ Having adequate knowledge prior to making the leap into a venture like this can help you avoid the pitfalls that can befall some new real estate investors. Getting into real estate investing can be exciting and lucrative, but you have to be willing to deal with the negatives as well as the positives.

❖ Have realistic goals and remember that real estate investing is a process. Those who claimed to have gotten their wealth quickly through real estate investing probably don't have it now.

❖ Even in downtimes, you can still profit. There will always be people that are looking for a place to live.

❖ After you feel comfortable with the first one, then you may want to look for the next one, and so on. This will help you to appreciate your investments better as opposed to being in a hurry to make money and acquire wealth.

❖ Getting the right tenant for your properties can sometimes be a hassle. However, it's better to take your time and get the right people so you can avoid a major headache later.

❖ It takes a lot to maintain and manage real estate properties. When you get to the point where you have a nice cash flow every month, you can hire a property management company to do the work for you. This will free you from the tasks that you would get used to doing yourself. That would include getting rental payments and dealing with various tenant issues.

❖ Since you are not Superman, don't expect to do all of

the repairs yourself. There may be some minor cosmetic issues you can take care of. Other than that, leave it up to the professionals.

❖ In addition to repairs, you will need to keep enough funds on hand in order to honor your mortgage loan obligations on time.

❖ Try to keep an open mind and don't get yourself worked up when things go wrong, as they will when you have tenants. If you do your homework, you can avoid some of the issues that can happen to investors.

❖ You will be able to increase rent as time goes on. This will help you produce a cash surplus while you are still paying the same amount on your mortgage loan. This of course, can happen if you have a structured loan payment that doesn't fluctuate during any given period.

❖ Be better than your competition. Don't just put up a sign and hope that people will come. You have to market and advertise. You may need to place ads in the paper and get with seasoned real estate professionals to help you.

❖ Eventually you will have so many investment properties that you won't have a choice but to hire a property management company to take over. Of course, you will have to set aside funds to pay them for their services. That's all the more reason for you to take it easy when it comes to building wealth with real estate investments.

You will be successful once you employ strategies that take you from one step to the next. It's better to have properties that will provide you with a steady income rather than waiting on the next blockbuster that may take years to come.

About The Authors

Business owner, entrepreneur, philanthropist, husband and father, Tim Johnson started his first company at the age of 24, which included designing a new product and acquiring investment capital necessary to finance the company's operations. Shortly thereafter he started his next company and eventually created enough capital to get him into the real estate business. He spent the next few years working with investors from all over the country, and he would share with these investors his methods of investing in real estate.

Tim has always been interested in real estate and real estate financing. In 2010 he started his own property management company, Bradley Management, LLC, which Janelle runs. This company grew very quickly and provides a variety of services to investors all over the world.

Tim is now involved with the development and growth of the exciting personal development and branding company called The Market Maker Group, LLC. Having created a considerable on line brand and professional presence, Tim realized every individual needs their own mark. Tim understands the importance of creating, maintaining and defending your reputation, and is dedicated to helping every individual meet those needs.

Bradley Management, LLC is an Indiana based company established in 2010 that helps investors throughout the world invest, renovate and manage real estate.

The company uses its personnel's vast experiences to provide a wide variety of services for its customers so that all their needs are met in the real estate market. Bradley Management has a reputation for meeting those needs and, therefore, the company has grown accordingly. The Market Maker Group provides an aid to businesses to help them reach their marketing goals.

For more information on Tim, Janelle and their services, check out **Yourpropertyresourcecenter.com** and **bradleymanagementgroup.com,** or contact Tim directly at **tim@bradleymanagementgroup.com.**

Chapter 16

The Most Important Business Book.....Yours
by Mike & Carolyn Lewis

We're not in the information age any longer. Social media has brought us into the referral age, or as my good friend Glenn Dietzel says:

" into the age of the recommendation".

I would like to start off with a question: *What is the most important business book ever written?*

The most important business book ever written is.... the one with your name on it!

Would you like to be able to do one simple thing that will totally change the way your customers perceive you? Would you like to have a product that not only sells with a big profit margin, but is also the platform on which you can build all of your other larger and more profitable products that will help you and your business?

Wouldn't it be fun to do something that will shock the heck out of all your friends and family?

The Long Hard Road

Up until two years ago I had a career as a very successful land developer. I owned and operated a $100 million building and development company that built projects throughout the southeastern United States.

You could say that I was living the American Dream.

We had big houses in each state, fancy cars, several boats, and flew by private plane.

My wife and I took exotic vacations at a moments' notice.

Then everything changed.

I had gone from making as much as $1 Million dollars in one day, down to being unable to make enough money to pay my family's monthly obligations.

I found myself in an economy worse than I had ever faced before, and I ended up losing my entire business, plus filing a $60 Million bankruptcy.

Here I was in my mid-50's and for the first time in my life with no job and no income.

I considered my options. I had already done the real estate seminar circuit almost 30 years ago, but didn't think that anyone would want to pay to listen to how they could turn $100 Million of assets into $6 cash!

It was painfully obvious that the industry I'd spent my entire lifetime becoming an expert in would not be back for at least 10 years... If it ever comes back!

So now I was forced to go out and find another way to make a living.

I looked for other work to do, but frankly, given my age and my experience, I wasn't qualified for most of the jobs that were out there. So I researched my other options, and decided that I could learn to make money on the internet.

I chose to get involved in Internet marketing because it looked like it had unlimited growth, and it didn't matter what age you were or what your background was. All that mattered was what you could do today.

After struggling for two years barely making a living, I looked to see what it was that the successful people in the marketplace had that I didn't have.

The answer that I found was that they had **trust** and *authority*!

Hard work and a good product just wasn't enough in this marketplace: you need to have both the authority and the trust necessary to convince buyers that your product is the ONE they want to purchase.

The more I studied the successful people in the marketplace, the more often I found that the one major thing they all had in common was that they had became published authors. Each one of them could point to a drastic change in their career once they had published and started to be perceived as an authority in their area.

So I decided that I needed to do what 99.9% of people don't or can't do - become a published author, too. There were just a couple of problems: One was that I needed it done right away, when it typically takes years to write a book, and secondly, I wasn't sure that I had it in me to write a book.

But I was determined to find a way to become a published author. I knew the added trust and authority was what I needed to get me over the hump and to be able to start making a great living, and living the lifestyle that I wanted for my family.

The Power of the Written Word

For thousands of years authors have been regarded with respect and admiration. And since they wrote the book, one word always came to mind....expert.

Authors tend to find themselves in the crowd that is the "cream of the crop". Being an author is the definitive demarcation line of attack, as it truly separates you from the pack. Whether you decide to write your own book, use a ghostwriter, or be included in a Multi Author book with other leaders, there's no better way for you to create yourself as an authority. Once your potential customers realize that you are a published expert, they will be ready to work with you, as well as refer others.

Most authors do not write their books for the money. Believe it or not, there really is very little money in books, unless you are a J.K.Rowling, or Donald Trump. In the real world of book writing, the actual purpose isn't the book. It's all about what the book **will do for you**. It's all about the new opportunities that will be created, as well as all the doors that will finally open for you.

Let's explore some of the concrete benefits that becoming a published author will afford you:
- New-found respect and admiration
- Personal satisfaction
- Enhanced credibility
- Expert status with your customers
- New customer surge due to your increased credibility
- Businesses, opportunities, and people naturally seek you
- High sense of accomplishment

- Newfound connections and increased earnings

Can you see the awesome benefits that being an author will afford you? Being an author can double, triple, or even quadruple your chances of getting every customer you meet as a client. You'll profit from being an author for your entire life. And no one can take that away from you.

Look around you. Have you ever noticed how authors kind of seem to "strut their stuff"? Call it confidence! They tend to carry themselves a little bit differently because they, as well as others, perceive them as different. It's not ego, but the knowledge that they are viewed differently because they are the expert in their field.

Credibility and esteem are what give authors this little "strut". This is an invaluable tool, which used properly, can translate into $$$. When your customers trust their source, it makes it possible for them to make important decisions in their business.

The trust and authority granted to authors is already formed in the minds of the public, as well as the media. This knowledge is worth more than a king's ransom! This knowledge should be the foremost reason for becoming an author. Like we stated earlier, it's all about the new opportunities, the previously closed doors opening, and enhanced business relationships that being an author creates. All this answers the question of "Why should I become a published author"?

Think about it. Would you rather work with an "Average Joe", or an "Author/Expert"? Of course you'd rather do business with the expert. So would the majority of the population.

Writing a book will allow you to STAND OUT from your competition....and put you at the level of all the other leaders that you have admired.

Let me tell you about one of our success stories:

> *Dave was a little leery about how the power of a book would change his career, as well as his life. After many conversations, we finally convinced Dave to let us do a book for him. The day after he received his published books, he was one of three contractors bidding on a very prestigious job.*
>
> *Dave decided to go all out and see if what we'd been telling him was true. So when he walked into the conference room, he proceeded to hand out his book to the Project Manager and a few others that were there.*
>
> *He felt the interview went well, but was quite shocked when 20 minutes into the interview they immediately hired him.*
>
> *A few days later he had asked the Project Manager how his presentation differed from the other candidates. The answer shocked him. The PM said "We are a billion dollar company. Money is really no object to us, so money was not really the issue when we decided to hire someone. You were the only one who came in to the interview with their own book. This showed us that you had knowledge about your field, took pride in your work, and that you were the*

expert that we needed". He went on to say that "the head of the division still had my book sitting on his credenza".

A year later, Dave is still working with the Company, hired more associates, gained more clients, and actually works less hours.

Do you think that Dave would have gotten the job if he didn't have his book? Maybe, maybe not. But we believe there is irrefutable proof that his credibility actually came from being a published author.

The bottom line is that being an author automatically makes you an expert. If you want an advantage over your competitors....then become a published author and brand yourself as the business expert in your niche.

There is no greater branding, or client enticement, than being a published author.

Become a published author today.

About Mike Lewis, "The Book Guy"

Mike has over 35 years of experience in marketing, finance, construction and real estate. He previously owned and operated several companies in the southeast, including a $100 million land development company.

He is the owner / publisher of Nomad CEO, the top Ghost Publishing firm in the world, specializing in books, tools, and resources for entrepreneurship and small businesses.

His products are practical, hands-on, and based on the real-world experiences of successful entrepreneurs, CEOs, investors, lenders, and seasoned business experts.

Mike's passion for turning non-writers into authors of printed books in less than 30 days, with virtually no writing on their part, positively impacts and changes lives.

Using his complete "Done For You" publishing service has helped raise his client-author's authority and recognition in all phases of their businesses.

Check out Mike's website at **www.nomadceo.com**, or contact him directly at **mlewis@nomadceo.com** for information on how you, too, can become the expert in your field through the power of becoming a published author.

About Carolyn Lewis, "The Book Diva"

Carolyn Lewis has the experience it takes to run a dynamic organization. From her first brush with the internet, to her management skills of launching AOL discs to your mailbox, and her ever increased move up the corporate ladder, this culminated as Chief Financial Officer of their $100million Land Development Company.

Carolyn has a diverse business background in such areas as finance, marketing, management, human resources and production, including owning and operating her own businesses.

After a diligent review of various business opportunities, the potential to impact people's lives with a published book was by far the most exciting choice. Coupled with the enjoyment she receives from working with other professionals, as well as the obvious choice that this was a great business model, convinced her that this is where she wants to be.

With a true passion and desire for helping entrepreneurs to "take it to the next level", Carolyn is here to assist you in producing your printed book, therefore accomplishing your goal to become the "best of the best" in your field.

Contact Carolyn directly at **clewis@nomadceo.com** for more information on how you, too, can join the ranks as a published author.

Visit us at **www.nomadceo.com**.

16657792R00082

Made in the USA
Charleston, SC
04 January 2013